Learning
CONSTRUCTION

GL
SPAN~ISH
^

A Beginner's Guide to Spanish *On-the-Job*

Spanglish/espanglés/inglañol n., 1. A form of
Spanish spoken on both sides of the U.S.—Mexico
border, and rapidly winning over (or poisoning,
depending on who you ask) the rest of the
Spanish-speaking world. 2. The natural mixing of
English and Spanish as people interact. 3. A fun
and sensible way of learning to communicate on
the job site. 4. The subject of this book (Duh).

Learning
CONSTRUCTION

SPANISH

A Beginner's Guide to Spanish *On-the-Job*

Terry Eddy

Alberto Herrera

Foreword by Ilan Stavans

McGraw-Hill

New York   Chicago   San Francisco   Lisbon   London
Madrid   Mexico City   Milan   New Dehli   San Juan
Seoul   Singapore   Sydney   Toronto

CONTENTS

CONTENTS

Appendices

Foreword

Ilan Stavans

¡Coooolísimo!

Delve into this charming handbook and, like me, you're likely to ask: Ooooops, wasn't English ever the unofficial "official" language of *los Unaited Estaits*? The *lecciones* in these pages are proof that it must have been long, long ago, a period that makes one think this nation was part of a galaxy far, far away. Spanglish is increasingly the lingua franca--*franquísima*, I would say--of the more than 40 million Latinos *de este lado del Rio Grande*. But not only Hispanics use it, so do the Anglos. It is *en todas partes*, anywhere and everywhere.

Slowly but surely, in the last one hundred and fifty years, this hybrid, which, like a margarita frozen with salt, adapts the damn flavors of the tropics to the tastes of the north, has made its way to kitchens and classrooms, news rooms and churches, advertising agencies and political pulpits. Yet in spite of its sustained history, many people are only now recognizing it as the new drink in town. In other words, Spanglish is finding its own space, which is why the title page of this volume tickles me: the letters *GL* force themselves into the word *Spanish*. Yeah, a cultural force we need to reckon with, to savor, to free it from its parenthesis.

Naturally, the purists are cringing. Why not teach *el español hecho y derecho*? In other words, whatever happened to linguistic purity--has it gone by way of the haywire? Try talking to construction workers in proper Spanish and see what happens. You won't get too far, I'm afraid. Immigrants don't move to *El Norte* to use their language reverentially, to safeguard it from the menacing Anglos. They're actually quite loose about it. The last thing in their mind is that syntax should be protected. Their priority is to make a living. Words, phrases--these are only tools to make themselves understood. And how do they use them? Much like a jazz musician, improvising as they go along, from *calma* to *rumba*. They acclimate to their circumstance, coining fresh terms, switching verbal codes, transposing and translating. The result is a hodgepodge of linguistic patterns: *naifa* for knife, *fremear* for to frame, *shiroke* for sheetrock. Or else, *tiene que traer un bonche de clavos*, you need to bring me a bunch of nails. Are these incorrect terms?

Yes, but so what?

Communication is the freest, most democratic of human endeavors. The effort to codify a language is essential since it establishes patterns and recognizes rules and regulations. In the end, though, its shape is up to its users. *The Canterbury Tales*, is that English? Yes, but in archaic form. How come it is so difficult to understand without the help of a scholarly apparatus? The answer is simple: languages exist in constant mutation. To remain useful, they need to borrow foreign terms, to create neologisms, to adjust to changing times. Indeed, Geoffrey Chaucer's English in fourteenth-century London was not unlike Spanglish today: a hybrid, influenced by the Romans, Saxons, and Normans. It would take a long time and geniuses like Shakespeare to acquire its current profile as the world's most important tongue. Likewise with Spanish: if good ol' Cervantes, to whom we owe the magisterial novel *Don Quixote of la Mancha*, came back from his *tumba*, would he know how to be a *cibernauta* while eating a burrito with salsa picante?

Well, he would need some *lecciones*. It would not be a stretch to give him this book, which is among the best in coping with the *realidad verbal* surrounding us. One might say that since Cervantes was a soldier and tax collector, he would find little connection to *la construcción*. Wrong!

I'm also not in the business and yet I found this beginner's guide is a *tour de fuerza* across a different type of construction: our national speech. Its mere existence will infuriate some. I, instead, am enthralled by its humor and easy-to-use strategies. I love the "dumb-looking symbols," the Gringo, the little carpintero, and the life ring that bails the reader out of difficult situations. Plus, what other language manual includes a glossary with words like *carajo*, *pinche* and *pendejo*? I've spent far too many hours opening textbooks that supposedly teach you this or that foreign tongue. They might look fancy but are often dry, obnoxious, insipid, and terribly frustrating. You do learn alright but, hey, did it cross anyone's mind that people need to have some fun too?

On further thought, maybe I'm in the wrong business. In construction, it appears, you talk, talk, talk in whatever way you can, and then, some months later, there's a building to show, proof that the act--and art--of communication was successful.

Say whaaaaat! Say *viva la jerga loca*!

Language is **speech**. In spite of what they tried to teach us in school, language really is not about grammar rules, spelling tests, or writing exercises—it's about communication. We all learned to talk, to communicate, years before anyone tried to teach us to read or write. In fact, there are millions of people in this world who can't read or write, but who can and do talk to each other. Language is arbitrary, that is to say it is nothing more than a collection of sounds that mean things because that's what we say they mean. So, what's the big deal about choosing the best way of learning a new language? Well, it all depends on what you plan on doing with it.

If you have a burning desire to learn Spanish so that you can travel the world, write a book about bull fighting, or read Don Quixote in the original (good luck with that, dude—it was written like 400 years ago, and Spanish was very different way back then), we advise you to enroll in your local college or university. For somewhere between $5,000 and $500,000, you can get your degree in Spanish, including grammar, spelling and the whole nine yards. On the other hand, if you are really just interested in learning to communicate in Spanish on the job site, we think you will find our method is faster, cheaper, and loaded with the kind of words you're really going to need—the words that are actually used in construction sites. We follow the common belief that everyone learns faster and remembers more when dealing with things which are important to them and which they use regularly.

How Is This Book Different?

Visit any bookstore, and you might find whole shelves full of books, tapes and CDs, all offering to teach you Spanish. Why does the world need another program, and what makes us think we have something to offer that somebody isn't already doing? To begin with, we listen to our audience—the building community. Many commercial Spanish programs are just great if you are planning a month's vacation in Madrid; you will learn how to get through customs, hail a cab, check into your hotel, and order what you want from a restaurant menu. This is all great stuff, but not very helpful when what you need to say has more to do with pouring footings, framing, plumbing, or roofing a building. The success of our job site bilingual dictionary, *Constructionary™/Construccionario™*, which focuses only on construction terms, demonstrates that people like you are looking for language tools that are practical and useful.

We are also not going to beat you to death with all ten different tenses of verbs in Spanish, the way other programs insist on doing. We'd love to do away with verbs completely if we could; unfortunately, verbs are the action words in any language (do, make, dig, lift, move, come, go, etc.), and nothing makes any sense without them. This program will teach you three basic time tenses—past, present, and future. With the use of these three, you will be able to speak Spanish in the job site and be understood, and that is our goal.

Let's talk about communication in plain English. We think you will agree that most of what you need to communicate on a construction job site can be said using only the past, present and future of English verbs ("I already did it", "I'm doing it right now", and "I'm going to do it later"). Spanish is no different. In fact, basic communication is possible using only the present tense. Most of you interested in this program have worked, or are working around individuals who are just learning English. When you hear someone say "I go to the doctor yesterday", or "I do that tomorrow", you understand what they mean, right? They used the present tense verb for the past or future, but you got the point. When learning a foreign language this is

O.K., since the first goal is to get across the idea. Remember, our goal is speech communication.

SPANGLISH

Most Spanish language programs also fail to recognize that there is no one Spanish language to begin with (in spite of what the Royal Spanish Academy may think). Just as the English, Scottish, Irish, Canadians, Americans, Aussies, New Zealanders, and South Africans all claim to speak something called English, but each in their own particular way, every Spanish-speaking country has its own spin on the language. Where Argentina has picked up accents and words imported by thousands of Italian, German and English immigrants, Mexican Spanish has adopted more than 50,000 words from the Aztecs and other native groups who were there when the Spaniards arrived. Because the United States has one of the largest Spanish-speaking populations in the world, we continue to develop our own unique dialect, blending English and Spanish into what is generally called Spanglish. So what is Spanglish, and how is it different from textbook Spanish? Here are two of the main differences:

If you listen closely to native Spanish speakers in the U.S., you will note that they frequently go back and forth between English and Spanish, even in the same sentence. Even though they seem to be speaking Spanish, you will hear words such as mall, grocery store, drug store, computer, mouse, hamburger, french fries, soda, and hundreds of other English words. It's not that Spanish doesn't have words for all these things, but since so much of our society functions in English, it is just easier to use the English word instead of the Spanish one (for instance, "mouse" is "dispositivo apuntador" in Spanish, which nobody uses it, although it is correct). But before you start thinking there is something strange about that, it might interest you to know that you already speak some Spanglish yourself. For, example, when you go out for Mexican food, I'm

3

guessing that your order sounds something like, "I'll have the cheese **enchiladas**", rather than "I think I will have a couple of those omlette thingys with the cheese inside and the sticky red sauce on top". Right? Now consider this, we use freely the words **hacienda**, **pueblo**, **flamenco**, **gusto**, etc., we just say them with an English pronunciation. And when you make travel arrangements, I sure hope you tell the ticket agent that you want to go to **San Francisco** or **San Antonio**, because you won't get far trying to book yourself to Saint Francis, California, or Saint Anthony, Texas. We all learned these Spanish words, because everyone else uses them, and we toss them in just as if they were a natural part of the English language.

Because of the differences in accents and pronunciation between the two languages, many English words which started out being used as above, have actually been transformed into Spanish (actually Spanglish) equivalents, with many Spanish speakers often not even realizing that these words are not actual "Spanish" words in the sense of finding them in Spanish textbooks or dictionaries. A Coke® becomes a Coca, a roof becomes a ruffo, a yard becomes a yarda, tape (for which there really isn't a good Spanish word, anyway) becomes a teip, and so on. Yes, you can learn textbook Spanish and be understood, but if you really want to effectively communicate and understand the Spanish everyone else is speaking on the job site, getting a good grasp of Spanglish is definitely the way to go. We have thrown in lots of these kind of words, as well as hints on how to use the U.S. "dialect" to your advantage. To make it as easy as possible for you, we identify Spanglish words with a note in a special type style—*Spanglish*. That way, you can learn them if you want to, or ignore them if you want to be a purist.

Let's take a real live example of an everyday English sentence, how it would be in good, textbook Spanish, and then how it could be said in Spanglish. Here's our sentence:

4

"Pedro, please park the truck in the driveway".
"Pedro, por favor estaciona la camioneta en la cochera".

First, we'll break down the key parts (or words), comparing English and proper Spanish:

Pedro, / please / park / the truck / in the driveway

Pedro, / por favor / estaciona / la camioneta / en la cochera

Pretty much looks like a foreign language, right? Makes you wonder if you are nuts to even think about learning Spanish. Well, don't give up yet—let's see how this same sentence would come out using a little Spanglish:

Pedro, / please / park / the truck / in the driveway

Pedro, / por favor / parkea / la troca / en el drai-wey

O.K., Sherlock. I'm guessing that I don't have to give you too many clues here before you figure out that this is a whole lot easier. Let's even go a step further, and let you actually say this sentence, using the kind of easy phonetic pronunciation help we will be giving you throughout the book. Remember to stress (i.e., put the emphasis on) the syllables in capital letters.

Pedro, por favor parkea la troca en el drai-wey
PEH-droh phor fah-VOHR par-KEH-ah lah TROH-kah ehn ehl DRAH-ee-way

See—you haven't even started the first lesson, and you have already said something in Spanglish which you understand and can remember (because it is so close to English), and which Spanish-speaking workers are going to understand as well. It would probably get you an F- in high school Spanish, but who cares? This book is about communicating and being understood—no tests, no grades, no trips to the principal's office.

What to Expect

In choosing our program, you will be building useful vocabulary as you move through the building of a house. You will begin by learning the common words for materials, tools, and work needed for preparing and laying the foundation, and continue with framing, plumbing, wiring, roofing, etc., each one introducing additional words which you will need for those activities. If you are a trade specialist, you may want to just work on the sections which apply to your trade; if you are a generalist or a contractor, you can start with what you think you need most, and continue expanding your vocabulary as you see fit.

Throughout the book you will be seeing some dumb-looking symbols, so I guess we better explain them before you begin to wonder about our sanity.

Our little worried "Gringo" will appear whenever we throw you a curve that requires some explanation. All languages have some weird little quirks that seem perfectly normal to native speakers, but cause some heartburn to a new learner. Our guy is here to help you along.

Our happy little carpenter shortening a piece of lumber will be a sign that you are about to be treated to a shortcut which will help you learn to communicate better and easier. Why try to reinvent the wheel—shortcuts exist because somebody already found an easier way to do something.

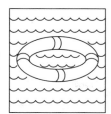

Even though our goal is to keep your learning experience as simple as is humanly possible, every once in a while things will unavoidably get really sticky, due to differences in the two languages. When this happens, we will throw you a life ring to help bail you out.

How to Use the Program

This is a program that lets you work at your own pace; we don't assign homework (who wants to grade all those papers anyway?). You can even skip around in the program if you want. That is what it makes this book unique -- you can use it any way that makes the most sense to you. However, our own clinical studies show that you will not learn much Spanish by putting the book under your pillow at night and sleeping on it. You need to read it, and practice using the words on the job, so your brain—or at least what's left of it--can begin to naturally connect each word with the actual object or action the word represents. Remember that we construct our own reality by naming things, so go forth and start learning the names in Spanish (or Spanglish) of the most common objects you use in your trade. In learning any new skill, such as driving nails or wiring a breaker panel for example, books or written instructions can help by giving basic directions (like, "Try to hit the nail, not your thumb, dummy!"). However, it is the practice, the constant repetition, which makes you a craftsman, not the instruction book. Learning a new language is like learning a new job skill—the more you practice, the better you get.

If there is any secret to learning to speak Spanish (or any other language, for that matter), it's that you have to dive right in and start using what you learn, even if you feel stupid at first. Maybe we shouldn't give away such a big secret right at the start, but there it is. Lesson number one (that's lección numero uno in Spanish, by the way) is that, to be understood, you don't have to be grammatically correct, or worry about great pronunciation. Close is good. Not so close will still get you by. The message doesn't even have to be all spoken—pointing or making motions like digging, sawing, etc., are all part of communication—they will help get your point across. And, using Spanglish, you are not going to wait until you can put full sentences together. Every time you learn another Spanish or Spanglish word for something, you are going to start using it in place of the English word. Your own personal Spanglish will start out being a whole lot more English than Spanish, which is O.K. However, as you work your way through this book, it won't be long before you are using more Spanish than English words in your sentences—and you will actually reach a point where you are comfortable regularly communicating in an effective and understandable form of Spanish.

START SPEAKING TODAY

You will be surprised to find how easily you can begin to communicate a lot of day-to-day stuff by just learning a few important words. Think about it. When you are speaking English on the job, how often do you communicate through only a couple of words instead of a long sentence. "Raise it", "Lower it", "Look out!", "Push!", "Pull!", etc. This works in Spanish too, so you can be well on your way to being job site bilingual without having to memorize a whole dictionary. Try these little gems for starters:

Definitions   Memory Hints

lo, los
[loh, lohs]

It, them   Let's face it, no one can learn all the words they need to know in the first week of trying a new language. So cheat! "It" and "them" work really well when you don't know the word for something, especially when you can point at whatever you are talking about. When written, the lo and los get tacked on to the end of the verb, as you will see below. (You probably don't need to know that, but I didn't want you to think I don't know what the space bar is for on my keyboard.)

sígame
[SEE-gah-meh]

Follow me.   From the Spanish verb **seguir** *[seh-GHEER]*, *to follow*. Very handy word to know. Instead of trying to remember enough Spanish to explain what needs to be done, use **sígame** to lead the person to where you need them to be, so that you can then point to or demon-

strate with words and hand gestures what
you want done.

levántelo
[leh-VAHN-teh-lo]

Lift it; raise it

> From the Spanish verb **levantar** *[leh-vahn-TAHR]*, *to lift*. This is a word you will use hundreds of times on the job site, whatever kind of construction work you do. Well worth remembering. To make it a plural "them", add an s, making it **levántelos**, lift them.

bájelo
[BAH-heh-lo]

Lower it, drop it down

> From the Spanish verb **bajar** *[bah-HAHR]*, *to lower*. See how your vocabulary is growing. You learn a few job site words, and already you know how Baja ("Lower") California got its name. How cool is that! Bájelos = lower them; drop them down.

jale
[HALL-eh]

Pull

> (Think: haul in English, which means to pull or drag something. Pronounced almost the same). From the Spanish verb **jalar** *[hah-LAHR]* or **halar** *[ah-LAHR]*, *to pull*. Can be used alone, **jale**, or as **jálelo**, **jálelos** (*Pull it, Pull them*).

empuje
[em-POO-heh]

Push

> From the Spanish verb **empujar** *[em-poo-HAHR]*, *to push*. For those of you who are paying attention, this is the opposite of **jale**. Can be used alone, **empuje**, or as **empújelo**, **empújelos**

(*Push it, Push them*). If you haven't been paying attention, you can stay after class and clean the erasers.

puche
[POO-shay]

Push

Even better, learn this *Spanglish* word, from the English, to push. Easier to remember than empuje, and will be understood by just about everyone. Use *púchelo, púchelos* for *push it, push them*.

un poco
[oon POH-koh]

A little, a bit, just a little

Real handy expression to use with **jale, puche, levántelo, bájelo**, and almost any other quick directions. Just add it onto the end—**levántelo un poco** (*Raise it a little bit*).

más
[MAHS]

More

Just like **un poco**, this can be added onto the end of directions (**bájelo más**—lower it more), or can be used as a one-word direction. For example, if you have already used something like **levántelo un poco**, and you need it raised further, just keep saying **más**, until it gets where you want it.

menos
[MEH-nohs]

Less

Works just like **más**. Use it at the end of directions, or all by itself.

un poco más/menos
[oon POH-koh MAHS/MEH-nohs]

A little more/less

> Anyone who didn't already get this one is definitely going to have to stay after class. I really just threw this in to show, once you've learned a few good words, it is really easy to start combining them.

bueno
[BWEHN-oh]

Good; O.K. Another handy word which you will find yourself using all the time. For example, think of a situation in which you need someone to lift a 2x4 and inch it into place so that you can nail it. Not hard to give understandable directions—**Levántelo** . . . **más**. . . **más**. **Un poco más**. . . **Bueno!** (Raise it up. . . more. . . more. A little more. . . Good!) Also used just like the English O.K. when someone asks for your permission or approval.

no
[noh]

No No means no in both languages, pronounced exactly the same way. To make it even easier, nodding your head means yes or O.K. in both languages, and shaking your head means no. Remember that gestures such as nodding, pointing or waving, are all a part of language, because they communicate something which the "listener" understands. Also, check out our note at the end of this section for a different use of no.

mire
[MEER-reh]

Look; pay attention; watch me; hey; yoohoo

> From the verb **mirar** *[Mee-RAHR]*, *to look, to look at, to watch*. This is a handy, and universally understood expression, which can be used to start sentences when giving instructions, relaying messages or information, or getting someone's attention.

oíga
[OY-gah]

Listen; listen up; pay attention

> "Yo, Adrian!" (Love those Rocky flicks!) From the verb **oír** *[oh-EAR]*, *to hear*. This works pretty much the same way as **mira**, in fact the two are almost interchangeable. **Mira** is used more, because you generally want the listener to look at you while you are talking, especially if you are trying to show him something.

cuidado!
[kwee-DAH-doh]

Be careful; watch it!

> This is used in much the same way as we would use Be careful! or Watch yourself! in English. When watching someone performing a task, you can say **cuidado!** as a general comment, or you can use it in a sentence such as, **Cuidado con el vidrio** (Be careful with the glass).

ojo!
[OH-ho]

Watch carefully; pay attention; watch what you're doing

13

Ojo is the Spanish word for eye. It is very handy when you are working with someone else, and you need him to pay attention to what you are about to do. Also used to call someone's attention to what he is doing or is about to do. It is actually more of a command than a warning.

aguas!
[AH-gwahs]

Look out! Run for cover! Get out of there fast!

Watch your backside!

This is a stronger and more immediate expression than **cuidado** or **ojo**. The word actually means *waters!* (**agua** is the Spanish word for water), which may seem like a pretty goofy way to warn someone. However, most Spanish-speaking countries are in tropical climates, where flash flooding is a frequent occurrence. Yelling **aguas!** in these areas is much the same as yelling **fire!** or **bomb!** in other areas of the world. People immediately know to run. This expression is used to warn someone of immediate danger from any source (gas leaks, falling objects, approaching vehicles, collapsing structures, bad roach-coach food, ex-wives showing up, whatever).

wachelo!
[WATCH-eh-loh]

Watch out!; look out!

Pure *Spanglish*, from the English verb to watch, and pronounced pretty much the same. Recognized and used throughout the U.S., Mexico and Central America. In fact, if you forget and just yell "Watch out!" most every-

one will understand you. It is used the same
way as aguas! and in the same circumstances.

Bonus word

O.K.   Use it as is. It's universal language (especially
if our universe is the construction world).

Besides this last one, we have just given you 15 great
words to memorize (assuming you decide on *wachelo* instead
of aguas, and *puche* instead of empuje), words which you can
start using immediately. We even told you how to pronounce them, or at least get close—remember, close is
good. O.K., who's that whining in the back of the class?
Give me a break here. When you were in the third grade,
old Miss Battleaxe used to give you 20 new spelling and
vocabulary words every week, and you handled that, didn't
you? So dig in, memorize and start using these—we guarantee you won't be sorry. And here comes the fun part;
once you have the ones you want memorized, and are
beginning to use them on the job, start thinking about all
the different combinations you can make out of them to
say even more. Check these out:

Ojo! *Púchelo* **un poco. Un poco más. Bueno!**
[OH-ho POO-cheh-loh oon POH-co. OON poh-co MAHS. BWEH-noh]

*Heads up! I need you to push that a little. A little more.
Good!*

**Mire. Levántelo.   Menos. No, levántelo un poco más.
Bueno!**
*[MEE-reh. leh-VAN-teh-loh. MEH-nos. No. leh-VAHN-teh-lo oon POH-coh
MAHS]*

Hey. Lift that for me. Down. No, now raise it a little. Good!

Cuidado! Bájelos. Más. Más. *Wachelo! O.K.!*
Careful. Lower them. More. More. Look out! O.K.!

Oiga. Sígame. Ojo.
Listen up. I need you to follow me. Watch where you're going.

You will notice that many of your Spanish-speaking fellow workers have a habit of ending a lot of sentences with "no?" Be careful here, they are not adding "no?" to deny what they just said. In this case, "no?" is Spanish shorthand for **¿no es verdad?** ("isn't that right?"), making it more of a yes than a no in translation. It is exactly the same as ending English sentences with right? or O.K.? This may seem strange at first, but trust me here, it is addictive. As you pick up and use more Spanish, you are going to find yourself ending most of what you say with "no?" just like everyone else.

SECTION I

Lesson 1: Who, What, How?

ME TARZAN, YOU JANE
(Personal Pronouns, Articles, Nouns and Verbs)

Knock, Knock. . . Who's There? (pronouns)

Language is a way of using sounds to deliver a message. For the message to be understood by the recipient (the "listener"), it needs to at least tell who and what the message is about. Of course, it also helps when you can add some other useful details such as where?, when?, why?, how?, or how much?, and we will get to those words as we go along. To get started, let's look at the who, in English and Spanish:

Singular		Plural	
I	**Yo** *[yoh]*	*We*	**Nosotros** *[noh-SOH-tros]*
You	**Usted** *[oo-STEHD]*	*You*	**Ustedes** *[oo-STEHD-ehs]*
He *She*	**Él** *[ehl]* **Ella** *[EH-yah]*	*They*	**Ellos, ellas** *[EH-yohs, EH-yahs]*

O.K., let's have a little chat about the word "you" in Spanish. I am giving you **usted**, the correct, formal, all-purpose word. You will hear workers at times using **tú**, and even sometimes using **vos**. Not to worry; briefly, here's the name of that tune: **Usted** is, as I said, the "formal" you word. It is absolutely required in most circumstances, and is always correct, even when not required. You simply can't go wrong using **usted**.

Tú is a "familiar" or informal you word, and **vos** is an alternative to **tú** that, although not actually good Spanish, has taken on a life of its own in some Latin American countries. They are optional—never required—and are typically used only when speaking to children, family members and intimate friends. **Tú** also shows up in "churchy" language, as the equivalent to our thee, thy, thine kind of old, weird English. But, unless you are planning to stop work for daily prayer meetings, you probably don't need to know that bit of **tú** trivia.

There is a cultural/historical aspect to this whole **usted/tú/vos** thing that you need to know about. In years gone by, owners, bosses, and even rich homeowners in Latin America (i.e., the "masters") used to talk down to their employees and servants by using the **tú** form as if they were children, while demanding their workers and servants show them respect by always answering in the formal **usted** form. This dying practice is only kept in some regions between elders and children, but here's the thing—as a non-native Spanish speaker, using the **tú** (or **vos**) form may be taken by native speakers as a sign of disrespect, so why take the chance?

And, last but not least, this book is about learning to effectively communicate in the simplest way possible. You have to learn **usted**, because it is often required, while you don't really need the others (remember, they are purely optional), and trying to master them means one additional ending for every verb you need to learn. I'm guessing that in itself is reason enough to pass on them. Right? Learning **usted** is the perfect shortcut for all "you"-based needs.

Spanish verbs don't use "to" as a way of recognizing the base form—in fact, English is pretty much the only western European language that does. Spanish uses single words for the base verbs, and changes the ending on each to identify who the action is about. Jumping right into useful job site words, we take the Spanish verb **necesitar,** to need, or to need to, as an example. **Necesitar** (neh-seh-see-TAHR) is the base verb, the infinitive, the idling engine. To put it into action, you drop the **–ar** from the end, leaving **necesit-**, and then add the following:

Yo **necesito**   *I need, I need to*   necesit + **o**
[yoh neh-seh-SEE-toh]

Usted **necesita**   *You need, you need to*   necesit + **a**
[oo-STEHD
neh-seh-SEE-tah]

El/ella **necesita**   *He/she needs,*
[ehl/EH-yah   *or needs to*   necesit + **a**
neh-seh-SEE-tah]

Nosotros
necesitamos   *We need, we need to*   necesit + **amos**
[noh-SOH-tros
neh-seh-see-TAH-mos]

Ustedes
necesitan   *You guys need,*
[oo-STEHD-ehs   *or need to*   necesit + **an**
neh-seh-SEE-tahn]

Ellos/ellas
necesitan   *They need,*
[EH-yohs/EH-yahs   *they need to*   necesit + **an**
neh-seh-SEE-tahn]

We have listed six "who" possibilities, but if you look carefully, you will see that there are only four endings to remember. Both "you" and "he/she" in the singular take the same ending of **a**, and "you"/"they" in the plural takes the same ending of **an**. Those of us who continue to lose brain cells as we get older really appreciate these little shortcuts. "Let's see—all I have to remember is **o, a, amos, an**. I think I can handle that."

Bear with me here. There is one more little tidbit of verb info I need to give you before we move into how you can use all this quickly and easily on the job site. In English, we often use more than one verb in a sentence in order to get our message across, such as: I **need** (first verb) **to go** (second verb) to the lumberyard. When we use two verbs like this, only the first one is changed to identify who, while the second stays in the infinitive (the "idling" form). Spanish works much the same way, so the quickest way to start communicating job site directions in Spanish is to memorize the present tense of the verb **necesitar**, which we just covered. Here it is again:

Yo necesito   *I need, I need to*
[Yo neh-seh-SEE-toh]

**usted/él/ella
necesita**   *You, he, she needs or needs to*
[oos-TEHD, ehl, EH-yah
neh-seh-SEE-tah]

**Nosotros
necesitamos**   *We need, we need to*
[noh-SOH-tros
neh-seh-see-TAH-mos]

**Ustedes/ellos/
ellas necesitan**   *You (plural), they need or need to*
[oos-TEH-dehs/EH-yohs/
EH-yahs neh-seh-SEE-tan]

And, to add a simple finishing touch, remember the general Spanish word for "it", which is **lo**, and the plural **los** for "them". You did memorize these in the first one of the **Quickies**, didn't you? (For you more advanced folks, yes, there is **la** and **las** but don't worry about gender now. Using **lo, los** you 'll get your point across.) Once you can use these forms of to need, you only have to remember the infinitive form of other verbs in order to communicate or give directions. Check this out:

Yo necesito clavar el montante.   *I need to nail the stud.*
[Yo neh-seh-SEE-toh kla-VAHR ehl
mohn-TAHN-teh]

OR, even easier,

Yo necesito clavar<u>lo</u>.   *I need to nail it.*
[Yo neh-seh-SEE-toh kla-VAHR-lo]

**Usted necesita
usar los guantes.**   *You need to use the gloves.*
[oo-STEHD neh-seh-SEE-tah
oo-SAHR los GWAN-tehs]

OR, even easier,

Usted necesita usar<u>los</u>.   *You need to use them.*
[oo-STEHD neh-seh-SEE-tah oo-SAHR-los]

Juan necesita ayuda.   *Juan needs help.*
[whoAHN neh-seh-SEE-tah ah-YOU-dah]

Él necesita levantarlo.   *He needs to lift it.*
[EL neh-seh-SEE-tah leh-van-TAHR-lo]

Nosotros necesitamos cortarlo.   *We need to cut it.*
[no-SOH-trohs neh-seh-see-TAH-mos
kor-TAHR-lo]

Ustedes necesitan traer las vigas.
[oo-STEHD-ehs neh-seh-SEE-tahn trah-EHR las VEE-gahs]

You guys need to bring the joists.

Ustedes necesitan traerlas.
[oo-STEHD-ehs neh-seh-SEE-tahn trah-EHR-las]

You guys need to bring them.

Ellos necesitan medirlos.
[EY-yohs neh-seh-SEE-tahn meh-DEER-los]

They need to measure them.

Here is a little secret to cutting down your sentences even further. Because the who in Spanish is already pretty much identified by the **o, a, amos, an** endings, you only have to say the who when you are talking to someone about someone else. Here's how it works. When I say necesito, I don't have to say **yo**, because the **o** ending already told everyone I am talking about myself (remember, **yo necesito**). The same is true of we; the **amos** ending already tells everyone I am talking about we. Also, If I am talking to you about what I need you to do, I don't need the **usted**, because when I say necesita, the **usted** (you) is understood. So far--so good, but remember that the **a** ending in the singular could also mean he or she, and the **an** in the plural could mean them instead of you, right? So here's how that works; if I am talking to <u>you</u>, but about something I want <u>someone else</u> to do, then and only then do I need to throw in **el** or **ellos**, to make it clear that I may be talking <u>to</u> you, but I'm talking <u>about</u> someone else. Demo time:

Necesit<u>o</u> clavarlo.
[neh-seh-SEE-toh kla-VAHR-lo]

I need to nail it.

Necesita clavarlo.   *You* need to nail it.
[neh-seh-SEE-tah kla-VAHR-lo]

Él necesita clavarlo.   *(I'm telling you that)*
[EHL neh-seh-SEE-toh   ***he*** *needs to nail it*
kla-VAHR-lo].

Necesitamos clavarlo.   *We* need to nail it.
[neh-seh-see-TAH- mohs kla-VAHR-lo]

Necesitan clavarlo.   *You* ***guys*** *need to nail it.*
[neh-seh-SEE-tahn kla-VAHR-lo]

Ellos necesitan clavarlo.   *(I'm telling you that)*
[EH yohs neh-seh-SEE-tohn   ***They*** *need to nail it.*
kla-VAHR-lo]

Pretty neat, huh? You can use two-word or three-word sentences and be clearly understood. This is not only easier, but actually more correct. Native Spanish speakers never use a pronoun (yo, usted, él, etc.) unless it is absolutely required to make it clear who is doing/getting the action.

. . . And, Away We Go!

Here's what you paid your money for (see, we do remember). The following pages are going to break all this down into some of the logical steps in building a house. If you are a specialist, you may want to only concentrate on the parts you need; general contractors and other generalists will most likely want to take some time to get a good handle on the whole enchilada (sorry, I couldn't resist that one). Remember, it's your book, so you are the one making the decisions here. O.K., O.K., I know you're excited, so turn the page already!

But wait! How about a second Quickie before we go on?

YOU SAY TOMAATO AND I SAY TOMAHTO

Now that you have had the chance to practice some sentences with a little phonetic help, we thought this might be a good time to go over basic Spanish pronunciation. Just like English, there is a way of pronouncing the letters one at a time as you say the alphabet, and some differences in how you pronounce the same letters when they are a part of various words. However (and this is good news), there are no irregularities in Spanish pronunciation. Once you know how a letter is pronounced, you can depend on it—unlike English. We don't expect you to immediately memorize all of the following, but now you will know where to find it when you have a question about pronunciation.

| Letter | 1. **Alphabet Pronunciation** |
| | 2. **Word Pronunciation** |

a   1. *[ah]* As in your doctor holding your tongue down with an ice cream stick and telling you to say **ah**.
       2. The same—always **ah**.

b   1. *[beh]* Real close to how we say the word bay in English.
       2. Just like English.

c   1. *[seh]* Not like English, where we sound like we say *see* instead.
       2. The letter c in Spanish, like English, has a hard **k** sound in front of the vowels a, o, and u; and it has an **s** sound in front of the vowels e and i. Check out some **c** words in English, and you will see what I mean. When in doubt, think about how you would pronounce the word in English, then use the same **k** or **s** sound in Spanish. Foolproof method.

d   1. *[deh]* Like how we say *they* in English. It's a softer sound.
2. Similar to English.

e   1. *[eh]* Like how we say the word *bet* in English. Tricky—takes some practice.
2. Does not sound like **e** in English. Sounds more like our **a**.

f   1. *[EH-feh]* Hey, at least it rhymes with the others.
2. Pretty much like the **f** in English words.

g   1. *[heh]* As if you are laughing.
2. Another letter like **c** that has a hard and a soft sound—think of how we pronounce **g** in "Go" as opposed to "Gee whiz". In front of a, o, u, l, and r, the Spanish **g** is the same hard "Go" sound as is the English **g** in front of those same letters. In front of the letters e and i, the soft Spanish **g** sounds like hard English *h*. For example, the word **gente** (*people*) sounds *[HEHN-teh]*.

h   1. *[AH-cheh]* One for memorizing.
2. The letter **h** is **completely silent** in Spanish. Always; whenever you see an **h**, skip it, like in Cockney English, where "house and home" comes out like "'ouse and 'ome".

i   1. *[ee]* That's right—the Spanish **i** sounds like our **e**. Takes a while to get used to.
2. Always the same—*[ee]*.

j   1. *[HO-tah]* Did I say they'd all be easy?
You know that sound you make when you clear your throat? That's pretty much the sound of the letter **j** in Spanish. Sort of a really raspy **h** sound from the very back of your throat. Listen carefully to some native Spanish speakers and you will get the hang of it.

k 1. *[kah]* Think of the English **ca** sound in the word call.
2. Pretty much the **k** sound we use in English. Interchangeable with the hard **c** sound.

l 1. *[EHL-eh]* Close to how we Angelinos say "we're from L.A." (just cut the ee sound at the end).
2. Same sound as English.

ll 1. *[EH-yeh]* The "double l" is pronounced like our letter **y**.
2. Like the English letter **y**. For example, the Spanish verb **llamar** (*to call*) is *[yah-MAHR]*.

m 1. *[EHM-eh]* Close to what one of those sissy Hollywood types with the fake accent would say "I won an Emmy."
2. Like English.

n 1. *[EHN-eh]* These all begin to sound like talking pig Latin when we were kids, don't they?
2. Like English.

ñ 1. *[EHN-yeh]* Anytime you see this symbol, called a tilde, think of it as an **ny**.
2. Like the **ny** sound in English words like ca**ny**on and o**ni**on.

o 1. *[oh]* As the first sound of the word owe. (Don't close your lips to the oo sound! Stay in the first sound I say!)
2. Always pronounced as **oh** in Spanish—no variations like **ah** or **uh** that we sometimes get in English.

p 1. *[peh]* Sounds a lot like our word pay (no ee sound at the end though).
2. Pronounced like English **p** in words. Just be sure to watch any vowel which follows—the name Pedro is *[PEH-droh]*, not *[PEE-drow]*.

31

q   1. *[koo]* To get this letter in Spanish, lose the yew sound from English. It's *[koo]*, not *[kee-YEW]*.
2. Back-of-the-throat **k** or hard **c** sound.

r   1. *[EH-reh]* One of the toughest ones for us Gringos. To get it right, you need to roll it. Like when you used to play war as a kid, and you were the one with the machine gun. (Lucky you.) B-r-r-r-r-r-r-r-r. B-r-r-r-r-r-r-r.
2. Like the English **r** if that's the best you can do. Much better if you can roll it a little.

rr 1. *[EHR-rrreh]* Like **r**, but with a longer roll.
2. Again, just use the English **r**—you will most likely be understood, bad Gringo accent and all. Learning to roll your r's impresses native Spanish speakers, so give it some practice. It's not that hard.

s   1. *[EH-seh]* Like "I hate essay tests. Give me True and False questions, so I can cheat better!" Pronounced like the **s** in English.

t   1. *[teh]* Sounds like the first sound in **Tay**lor. Like English.

u   1. *[oo]* As in boot.
2. **oo** when it stands alone as a vowel, in words like cubre (cover)--KOO-breh. Silent after **q** as in **que** *[keh]*—what, or **quien** *[kyehn]*—who.

v   1. *[veh]* or *[beh]* Most Spanish speakers use the **v** and **b** sounds interchangeably for the letter **v**.
2. Either the English **v** or **b** sounds are O.K.

w   1. *[DOH-bleh-oo]* ("**double u**")
2. Only exists for foreign words—there are no words with **w** in pure Spanish. You can use the English pronunciation for Spanglish words like *wachear*.

x　**1.** *[EH-kees]* O.K., so you guys all know how to order a cold dos EH-kees, right? Good brew.
2. Most used as "**cs**" like in English for words as **conexión** *[coh-neks-SYOHN]* or **extensión** [eks-tehn-SYOHN]. Except in the word **México** *[MEH-hee-co]* and derivatives where it sounds like the Spanish letter **j**.

y　**1.** *[yeh]* or *[ee (gree-EH-gah)]* Called the "Greek i" in Spanish. The letter **i** is sometimes called *[ee lah-TEE-nah]*, the "Latin i".
2. Say it as the English **y**, and you will be safe. But be aware that you'll hear variations of it depending on the origin of the native speaker. That's why some folks end up in "Jail" when the intention was to place them in "Yale."

z　**1.** *[SEH-tah]* Note the **s** sound instead of the English **z** sound.
2. Always pronounced like our English **s**, so lose the **z**, Zorro. The sounds are close enough that, if you forget and use a **z** sound, you will still be understood.

33

Accents and Stress

Yeah, this whole thing is stressful, but that's not what we are talking about. Spanish has very definite rules about which syllable gets the emphasis—which one you stress. However, we aren't going to go digging around in ugly grammar rules for diphthongs, triphthongs, and the rest of that stuff. "Hold on," I hear you say, "What's all this about thongs?" Trust me, the kind you're interested in ain't got nothing to do with grammar—Spanish or English. Just go with the phonetic pronunciations we give you for all the words, and you'll do fine. Also, don't let accent marks throw you. All an accent mark does is to tell someone where to put the stress on certain words that don't follow the regular grammar rules. When you see an accent mark, you know where to put the stress—the emphasis. Can be really helpful at times.

Lesson 2: Foundations

FUNDACIONES

STEP ONE — NOUNS

English — Spanish
Notes and Memory Hints

trench — **zanja** *[SAHN-hah]*
> No simple way to remember. Either memorize it, or cheat and use zapata.

footing — **zapata** *[sah-PAH-tah]*
> Zapato is Spanish for shoe, which goes with "foot" in footing.

line — **línea** *[LEE-neh-ah]*
> Chalk line is línea de marcar—think "line for marking". Línea will do fine for both actual lines between stakes and lines chalked on the ground.

pick — **pico** *[PEE-koh]*
> Same word—different language (a "cognate")

shovel — **pala** *[PAH-lah]*
> Try naming your favorite shovel "Paula". That way, every time you think about using ol' "Paula", you will remember the Spanish word for shovel—**la pala**.

rake — **rastrillo** *[rahs-TREE-joh]*
> Memorization time again, although there is a *Spanglish* verb for "to rake" (see below), so you might try to use *la reka [REH-kah]* for rake.

depth — **fondo** *[FOHN-doh]*
> No cognate here. As a memory hint, associate it with related *fo-* words. You're digging down to put in the *forms* to pour the *foundation*.

width — **anchura** *[ahn-CHOORA]*
> Definitely one to memorize. Sorry. In a pinch, try using "distancia lateral" (lateral [or "side"] distance).

area — **area** *[AH-reh-ha]*
> Same as English; just watch the pronunciation.

STEP ONE — VERBS

English — Spanish
> **Notes and Memory Hints**

to follow — **seguir** *[seh-GEER]*
> Remember sígame from the first lesson? Same verb. Worth knowing.

to dig — **excavar** *[ex-kah-VAHR]*
> Think "to excavate" and you will do fine.

to rake — *requear* *[reh-keh-AHR]*
> Another great *Spanglish* verb. Say "rake" in English, add *eh-ahr* to the end and you've got it.

to level — **nivelar** *[nee-vehl-AHR}*
> Remember the **-vel** sound in both: *le-**vel**, ni-**vel***.

to measure — **medir** *[meh-DEER]*
> Memorize the little saying, "You must always measure, m' dear", and you will remember that *measure* = **medir**.

to use — **usar** *[oo-SAHR]*
> Cognate. Watch the pronunciation. It's "oo" like in "boot".

to clear — **limpiar** *[leemp-YAHR]*
> Memorize. Useful all around.

STEP ONE — SHAKE AND BAKE

. . . And away we go! With the use of necesitar, we can start mixing and matching some of these verbs and nouns to get some work done on our imaginary job site. Check these out:

Necesitamos excavar las zapatas.
[neh-seh-see-TAH-mohs ex-kah-VAHR las sah-PAH-tahs]
We need to dig the footings.

Necesita/necesitan limpiar el area.
[neh-seh-SEE-tah/neh-seh-SEE-tahn leemp-YAHR el AH-reh-ah]
You/you guys need to clear the area.

Necesita/necesitan seguir las lineas.
[neh-seh-SEE-tah/neh-seh-SEE-tahn she-GEER las LEE-neh-ahs]
You/you guys need to follow the lines.

Oiga! Necesito el pico.
[OY-gah. Neh-seh-SEE-toh el PEE-koh]
Hey! I need the pick.

Necesita usar la pala, no el pico.
[Neh-seh-SEE-tah oo-SAHR la PAH-lah, no el PEE-koh]
You need to use the shovel, not the pick.

Ojo. Necesita medir el fondo y la anchura.
[OH-ho. Neh-seh-SEE-tah meh-DEER el FOHN-doh ee la ahn-CHOOR-ah]
Watch it. You need to check the depth and width.

Necesita/necesitan nivelarlo.
[neh-seh-SEE-tah/neh-seh-SEE-tahn nee-vel-AHR-loh]
You/you guys need to level it out.

Necesita usar *la reka*.
[Neh-seh-SEE-tah oo-SAHR la REH-kah]
Use the rake.

Here's a time (and vocabulary) saver for measuring the depth and width of trenches. Until we get to numbers, tape measures, etc., you can easily demonstrate what you need by taking two stakes, marking one for the depth and writing "**fondo**" on it, the other for the width and writing "**anchura**" on it. These can be used by workers to continuously check depth and width as they dig. It ain't fancy language, but it works.

STEP TWO — NOUNS

English — Spanish
Notes and Memory Hints

stake(s) — **estaca(s)** *[ehs-TAH-kah]*
>Almost a cognate. For many English words starting with **s**, the Spanish word starts with **es**.

form(s) — *forma(s)* *[FOR-mah]*
>Definitely *Spanglish*. The actual Spanish word for concrete forms is **enconfrados**, but workers use and will understand **formas**.

board(s) — **panel(es)** *[PAH-nehl/PAH-nehl-ehs]*
>Think "panel", which can be a kind of board. The word **tabla** or **tablas** is also used, but **panel** is easier to remember.

rebar — **barra(s)** [BAH-rrah/BAH-rras]
>Easy to remember. Just think "bar" and "bars". Proper Spanish is **barras de refuerzo** (reinforcement bars), or **varillas**.

wire — **alambre** *[ah-LAHM-breh]*
>One to be memorized cold.

pliers — **pinzas** *[PEEN-sahs]*
>Think "pinchers", which is what some people

38

call pliers in English as well. The proper word
Alicates *[ah-lee-CAH-tehs]* is also used, in case
you hear it.

sledge hammer — **marro** *[MAH-rroh]*
> This is the real thing. A framing hammer is a
> martillo, a "little hammer."

STEP TWO — VERBS

English — Spanish
> **Notes and Memory Hints**

to put, to place — **poner** *[poh-NEHR]*
> Hey, at least they both start with p. Seri-
> ously, **poner** is one of the most used verbs in
> Spanish—a must-know.

to install — **instalar** *[ehn-stah-LAHR]*
> If you draw a blank on **poner**, this easy cog-
> nate will do for putting in forms and rebars.

to connect — **conectar** *[koh-neck-TAHR]*
> Can we say cognate, friends? There are other
> verbs such as **atar** *[AH-tahr]*, *to tie*, but this
> one is easier to remember.

to attach — **unir** *[oo-NEER]*
> Literally, "to unite", like when you are united
> in marriage, you are "attached" and not single
> anymore.

to bend — **doblar** *[doh-BLAHR]*
> Think "to double over", which requires bend-
> ing.

to twist — **torcer** *[tohr-SEHR]*
> Think torsion (like torsion wrench), which
> means twisting.

STEP TWO — SHAKE AND BAKE

Time to play our little version of connect the dots again, to see if we can get the right picture. Still using necesitar, we can now say such things as:

Necesita/necesitan poner las formas.
[neh-seh-SEE-tah/neh-seh-SEE-tahn poh-NEHR las for-MAHS]
You/you guys need to put in the forms.

Necesita usar el marro en las estacas.
[neh-seh-SEE-tah oo-SAHR el MAH-rroh ehn las ehs-TAH-kahs]
Use the sledge on the stakes.

Ojo. Necesitan unir los paneles.
[OH-ho. Neh-seh-SEE-tahn oo-NEER los pah-NEH-lehs]
You guys need to attach the boards.

Necesitamos poner (instalar) las barras.
[neh-seh-see-TAH-mohs poh-NEHR (ehn-stah-LAHR) las BAH-rras]
We need to put the rebar in.

Necesita doblarlo.
[Neh-sah-SEE-tah doh-BLAHR-loh]
(You need to) Bend it.

Necesita/Necesitan conectarlos.
[neh-seh-SEE-tah/neh-seh-SEE-tahn koh-neck-TAHR-lohs]
You/you guys need to tie them together

Necesita usar pinzas y alambre.
[neh-seh-SEE-tah oo-SAHR PEEN-sas ee ah-LAHM-breh]
Use the pliers and wire.

Mire. Necesita torcerlo.
[MEE-reh. Neh-seh-SEE-tah tohr-SEHR-loh]
Look. You need to twist it.

STEP THREE — NOUNS

English — Spanish
Notes and Memory Hints

foundation — **fundación** *[foon-dah-SYOHN]*
Pretty easy cognate to remember.

cement — **cemento** *[seh-MEHN-toh]*
Hard to miss this one—a true cognate.

concrete — **concreto** *[kohn-KREH-toh]*
A whole lot easier than the other Spanish
word for it—**hormigón** *[or-mee-GOHN]*.

sand — **arena** *[ah-REHN-ah]*
Careful, looks like our word *arena*, but <u>not</u> a
cognate.

mixer — **revolvedora** *[reh-vohl-veh-DOOR-ah]*
Think "to revolve", because that's basically
what it does. Also called a **mezcladora** *[mess-
klah DOH-rah]*; from the verb **mezclar**, *to mix*.

anchor bolt(s) — **perno(s)** *[PEHR-noh(s)]*
— **ancla(s)** *[AHN-klah(s)]*
Proper Spanish combines the two—**pernos de
anclaje**, but either **perno** (*bolt*) or **ancla**
(*anchor*) works fine, especially if you have a
sample to show.

sill plate — **placa** *[PLAH-kah]*
The actual Spanish term for the foundation
sill plate is a real mouthful, **placa de solera
de fundación**. Wow! *[PLAH-kah de...]*Never mind.
Stick with **solera** or **placa**, and point at it.

slab — **losa** *[LOH-sah]*
You'll need to memorize. Someone suggested
that *slab* and *slob* are close, as are **losa** and
loser, but I think that is stretching things a
bit.

trowel — **llana** *[YAH-nah]*
> **Llano** in Spanish means smooth. Think of
> Yanni as writing smooth music (I don't like his
> stuff, but the word association still works
> for me. *Yanni* = **llano** = *smooth*.)

STEP THREE — VERBS

English — Spanish
> **Notes and Memory Hints**

to pump — *pompear* *[pohm-pee-AHR]*
> Love those *Spanglish* words—they do make life
> so much easier.

to pour — **descargar** *[dehs-kahr-GAHR]*
> For descargar, think "discharge", which can
> mean to pour or dump something.

to wet (something) — **mojar** *[moh-HAHR]*
> **Mojado** means wet. But the Mojave Desert is
> dry as a bone. Go figure.

to "trowel", to smooth with a trowel
> — **allanar** *[ah-jahn-AHR]*
> — **aplanar** *[ah-plahn-AHR]*
> **Llano, plano** mean smooth or flat. Yanni time
> again. Smooth and FLAT!

to put in, to insert
> — **meter** *[meh-TEHR]*
> — **insertar** *[een-sehr-TAHR]*
> **Ojo!** Looks like English word meter, but
> doesn't mean the same, and is pronounced dif-
> ferently. Insertar works as an easier cog-
> nate.

to operate — **operar** *[oh-pehr-AHR]*
> Same verb in both languages—easy to remem-
> ber.

TIME TO ROCK AND ROLL AGAIN

Ojo. El necesita pompear el cemento.
[OH-ho. Ehl neh-seh-SEE-tah pohm-peh-AHR el seh-MEHN-toh]
Heads up. He's getting ready to pump some cement.

Wachelo! Necesitan descargar el concreto.
[WATCH-eh-loh! neh-seh-SEE-tahn dehs-kahr-GAHR el kohn-KREH-toh]
Watch it! They need to pour the concrete.

Necesitamos vaciar la losa.
[neh-seh-see-TAH-mohs vah-SYAHR la LOH-sah]
We need to pour the slab.

Necesita allanarlo.
[neh-seh-SEE-tah ah-jahn-AHR-lo]
You need to trowel it (to "smooth" it).

Necesitan poner los pernos (las anclas).
[neh-seh-SEE-tahn poh-NEHR los PEHR-nohs]
You guys need to put in the anchor bolts.

Necesita mojarlo.
[neh-seh-SEE-tah moh-HAHR-loh]
You need to wet it down.

DOWN FOR THE COUNT

Learning to count in Spanish is pretty easy. It is the same system we use in English, you just have to learn some new words for the numbers. Once you know how to count from one to twenty, the rest is repetition. Let's get started by knocking off the first set.

1-20

0 cero *[SEH-roh]*	
1 **uno** *[OO-noh]*	11 **once** *[OHN-seh]*
2 **dos** *[dohs]*	12 **doce** *[DOH-seh]*
3 **tres** *[trehs]*	13 **trece** *[TREH-seh]*
4 **cuatro** *[KWAH-troh]*	14 **catorce** *[kah-TOHR-seh]*
5 **cinco** *[SEEN-koh]*	15 **quince** *[KEEN-seh]*
6 **seis** *[seys]*	16 **dieciséis** *[dyeh-see-SEYHS]*
7 **siete** *[SYEH-teh]*	17 **diecisiete** *[dyeh-see-SYEH-teh]*
8 **ocho** *[OH-choh]*	18 **dieciocho** *[dyeh-SYOH-choh]*
9 **nueve** *[NWEH-veh]*	19 **diecinueve** *[dyeh-see-NWEH-veh]*
10 **diez** *[DYEHS]*	20 **veinte** *[VEYN-teh]*

That wasn't too bad, was it? Except for those teens, which look like a real mouthful. Actually, starting with sixteen, they used to be written like this: diez y seis (ten and six), diez y siete (ten and seven), etc. However, they get crammed together into one word when pronounced, so some genius came up with these one-word "phonetic" spellings. Same as English, where the word teen comes from ten, so we really say six and ten, seven and ten, etc.

20-30

20 veinte [VEYN-teh]	
21 veintiuno [veyn-TYU-noh]	26 veintiseis [veyn-tee-SEYS]
22 veintidós [veyn-tee-DOHS]	27 veintisiete [beyn-tee-see-EH-teh]
23 veintitrés [veyn-tee-TREHS]	28 veintiocho [veyn-TYOH-choh]
24 veinticuatro [veyn-tee-KWAH-troh]	29 veintinueve [veyn-tee-NWEH-veh]
25 veinticinco [veyn-tee-SEEN-koh]	30 treinta [TREYN-tah]

Now that we got through those, we can really roll. The numbers from thirty to ninety-nine are pretty repetitious, like they are in English. The only ones you really have to learn are thirty, forty, fifty, etc. You already know the one through nine to add on as you count.

30-100

30 treinta [TREYN-tah]	50 cincuenta [seen-KWEHN-tah]
31 treinta y uno [TREYN-tah ee OO-noh]	51 cincuenta y uno [seen-KWEHN-tah ee OO-noh] etc.
32 treinta y dos [TREYN-tah ee dohs] etc.	60 sesenta [seh-SEHN-tah]
40 cuarenta [kwar-EHN-tah]	61 sesenta y uno [seh-SEHN-tah ee OO-noh} etc.
41 cuarenta y uno [kwar-EHN-tah ee OO-noh] etc.	70 setenta [seh-TEHN-tah]

71 **setenta y uno** *[seh-TEHN-tah ee OO-noh]*	90 **noventa** *[noh-VEHN-tah]*
72 **setenta y dos** *[seh-TEHN-tah ee dohs]* **etc.**	91 **noventa y uno** *[noh-VEHN-tah ee OO-noh]* **etc.**
80 **ochenta** *[oh-CHEHN-tah]*	100 **cien** *[SYEHN]*
81 **ochenta y uno** *[oh-CHEHN-tah ee OO-noh]* **etc.**	101 **ciento uno** *[SYEHN-toh OO-noh]* **etc.**

You need to note that **veinte** ends in the letter **e**. When combined with **i** or **y,** the strong sound is the **ee** in saying 21 through 29. The words for 30 through 90 all end in the letter **a** instead of **e**. When you put a and y together, they both get pronounced— ah ee. To check your pronunciation, the two together should sound a little like the English word eye. Like treint-EYE-uno, ochent-EYE-cinco, etc. Also, note that by itself 100 is **cien**, but when you add additional numbers (101, 150, etc.), 100 becomes **ciento.** Not a real biggie—if you say ciento for 100 by itself, people will most likely forgive you.

200-1000

There are only a couple of special cases here, which we have put in bold type to help you recognize them. The rest are repetitions of what you have already learned.

200 doscientos	600 seiscientos
300 trescientos	700 **setecientos** *[seh-teh-SYEHN-tohs]*
400 cuatrocientos	800 ochocientos
500 **quinientos** *[kee-NYEHN-tohs]*	900 **novecientos** *[noh-veh-SYEHN-tohs]*
1000 mil *[meel]* **2000 dos mil, etc.**	

FREIMEANDO

STEP ONE — NOUNS

English — Spanish
> **Notes and Memory Hints**

frame/the framing — **estructura** *[ehs-truk-TOOR-ah]*
> Think "structure" for this one. *Structure*/
> **estructura** is a cognate.

framer   — *fremero* *[freh-MEHR-oh]*
> Pure *Spanglish*. Easy to remember.
> — **carpintero** *[car-peen-TEH-roh]*
> **Carpintero** will work if you are trying to avoid
> the easy *Spanglish*.

addition — **expansión** *[eks-pan-SYOHN]*
> Logical—an addition expands the building. You
> can get by with adición, a cognate which will
> be understood.

floor   — **piso** *[PEE-sah]*
> — **(el)** *flor* *[flohr]*
> How about memorizing: Please leave your dog
> outside the door so he won't "peeso" on my
> floor. Hey, if it helps you remember it . . .
> Seriously, most workers will recognize the
> *Spanglish* "*flor*" as long as it's *el flor* (**la flor** means
> *flower* in Spanish).

subfloor   — **subpiso** *[soob-PEE-soh]*
> — *subflor* *[SOOB-flor]*
> If you can get **piso** for floor, this should be a
> no-brainer. Otherwise, use the *Spanglish subflor*.

sill plate — **placa** *[PLAH-kah]*
> The actual Spanish term for the foundation
> sill plate is a real mouthful, **placa de solera**

de fundación. Go with pointing at it and using just placa.

joist — **viga** *[VEE-gah]*
> One you'll have to memorize, but a good word to know. **Viga** means beam, and a joist is sometimes called a **vigueta**, a little beam.

floor joist — **viga del piso** *[VEE-gah dehl PEE-soh]*
> Anyone who didn't get **viga** and **piso** for this? Don't make me assign homework.

hammer — **martillo** *[mahr-TEE-yo]*
> Literally "little hammer". Sledge hammer is **marro**, the Big Kahuna of hammers. The "illo" ending in Spanish means a little one.

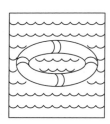

You already have a shovel named Paula, so name your hammer "Little Marty", and you will remember martillo.

saw — **sierra** *[SYEH-rrah]*
> You have seen this word before, no? Mountain ranges are called **sierras**, because all those peaks in a row look like saw teeth. What an education you're getting here!

nail(s) — **clavo(s)** *[KLAH-voh(s)]*
> The word is close to "clobber", which is what you are supposed to do to them, anyway.

board(s)
> — **panel(es)** *[PAH-nehl-(ehs)]*
> — **tabla(s)** *[TAH-blah(s)]*
> Think the English word panel, which is a kind of board. Works really well with plywood and

particleboard. **Tabla(s)** also means board(s), but **panel** is easier on the brain.

plywood — *triplay* *[TREE-plahy]*
Pure *Spanglish*, probably from the English "three-ply" and the Spanish word for triple.

STEP ONE — VERBS

English — Spanish
Notes and Memory Hints

to frame — *fremear* *[freh-MEAHR]*
Spanglish verb, goes with *fremero*. Doesn't get any better than this!

to measure — **medir** *[meh-DEER]*
Just memorize the rule, "You must always measure, m' dear", and you will remember this one.

to cut — **cortar** *[kohr-TAHR]*
Pretty close to a cognate—*cut* and **cort-** are very similar.

to put, place — **poner** *[poh-NEHR]*
For those of you just joining us for this session, poner is a must know verb—can't build or do much else without it.

to nail — **clavar** *[klah-VAHR]*
Goes with clavos (nails). You can't get much more basic than hammers and nails, so learn the words already! Clavar is even closer to "clobber".

to toenail — **clavar en ángulo** *[klah-VAHR en AHN-goo-loh]*
Thought I was going to forget this one, didn't you. Real men toenail their floor joists!

51

STEP ONE — SHAKE AND BAKE

If you skipped the foundation session (hey, it's your book, and we told you to use it any way you want) what we are going to do here is take the verb forms of necesitar, which we had you memorize, and combine them with this new vocabulary to see what works:

Necesitamos poner las vigas de piso.
[neh-seh-see-TAH-mohs poh-NEHR las VEE-gahs de PEE-soh]
We need to put in the floor joists.

Necesita/necesitan medir y cortarlos.
[neh-seh-SEE-tah/neh-seh-SEE-tahn meh-DEER ee kohr-TAHR-lohs]
You/you guys need to measure and cut them.

Mire. Necesita clavarlos en ángulo.
[mee-rehneh-seh-SEE-tah klah-VAHR-lohs ehn AHN-goo-loh]
Watch. You need to toenail them.

Ojo. Necesitan levantarlo un poco.
[OH-ho. neh-seh-SEE-tahn leh-vahn-TAHR-lohs oon POH-koh]
Heads up. You guys need to raise it up a little bit.

Necesitamos poner el subpiso.
[neh-seh-see-TAH-mohs pohn-EHR el soob-PEE-soh]
We need to put down the subfloor.

Necesitan la sierra, martillos y clavos.
[neh-seh-SEE-tahn la see-EHR-ah, mahr-TEE-jhos ee KLAH-vohs]
You're going to need the saw, hammers and nails.

Necesita cortar los paneles (el triplay).
[neh-seh-SEE-tah kohr-TAHR los pah-NEHL-ehs (el TREE-plahy)]
You need to trim the boards (the plywood sheets).

Bueno. Necesitan clavarlos.
[BWEH-noh. neh-seh-SEE-tahn klah-VAHR-lohs]
Good. You need to nail them down.

STEP TWO—NOUNS

English — Spanish
      Notes and Memory Hints

lumber — **madera** *[mah-DEHR-ah]*
> Literally, Spanish for "wood". You'll need memorize this one, or use **paneles** or **tablas**. One for those of you whose drinking habits go beyond beer: the Madera wine gets its flavor from wood aging.

stud(s) — **montante(s)** *[mohn-TAHN-teh(s)]*
> Think "mounting(s)", because that's really what they are—mountings to nail the sheetrock onto.

plate(s) — **placa(s)** *[PLAH-kah(s)]*
> Words like sill plate and top (rafter) plate can be a real mouthful in Spanish, but you can get by with just **placa**.

crosspiece(s) — **transversal(es)** *[trahns-vehr-SAHL-(ehs)]*
> If **placa** doesn't work for you, try this one, which is a cognate of the English for "transverse", or "crosspiece".

two-by-four(s) — **dos-por-cuatro(s)**
> *[dohs-pohr-KWAHT-roh(s)]*
> If you can count to twelve in Spanish, you can identify most lumber. If not, bribe your kids—they'll teach you if the price is right.

two-by-six(es) — **dos-por-seis(es)** *[dohs-pohr-sehs(ehs)]*
> See above. Use the sizes in Spanish just like in English.

four-by-four — **cuatro-por-cuatro**
> *[KWAT-roh-pohr-KWAT-roh]*
> See above.

four-by-twelve — **cuatro-por-doce** *[KWAT-roh-pohr-DOH-seh]*
> O.K., now I'm bored. I'm hoping you get it without a tour of the whole lumberyard.

power saw — **sierra eléctrica** [SYEH-rah ehl-EHK-tree-kah]
> Once you've got sierra for saw, **eléctrica** is a cognate of *electric*. Not too tough.

bunch — *bonche* [bohn-CHEH]
> Pure *Spanglish* and easy to remember. It's just the English word with a Spanish pronunciation.

wall — **muro** [MOO-roh] — **pared** [pahr-EHD]
> That's right, there are two of them, and neither one sounds like wall. For **muro**, think of a "mural", which is a painting on a wall. For **pared**, I think "partition" is a bit of a stretch, but if it works for you, go for it.

joint — **unión** [oo-NYOHN]
> Pretty easy—a joint is a union of two separate pieces. And to be fair to our readers in Dixie, there is also a good cognate *separation*/**separación** if union is a bad word in your family.

STEP TWO — VERBS

English — Spanish
> **Notes and Memory Hints**

to bring — **traer** [trah-EHR]
> Memorize it! There is no cognate or *Spanglish* equivalent. This is an important verb which you will use frequently.

to build — **construir** [kohn-strew-IHR]
> Like "to construct"—obviously a very important verb which you need to know.

to raise — **elevar** [eh-leh-VAHR]
> Think "elevate" and you've got it. If you forget, **levantar** will work in a pinch.

to position — **situar** *[seet-oo-AHR]*
> "To situate", which some of you may use
> already in English for positioning walls, etc.

to hold — **soportar** *[soh-pohr-TAHR]*
> There are a lot of words for "to hold" in
> Spanish, depending on who, what and how, but
> this cognate for "to support" works well for
> holding up beams and walls

STEP TWO — SHAKE AND BAKE

Necesitamos construir los muros.
[neh-seh-see-TAH-mos kohn-strew-EER lohs MOO-rohs]
We need to build the walls.

Juan, necesita medir y cortar los montantes.
[HWAHN, neh-seh-SEE-tah meh-DEER ee kohr-TAHR los mohn-TAHN-tehs]
Juan, you need to measure and cut the studs.

Necesitan clavar los montantes en las placas.
[neh-seh-SEE-tahn klah-VAHR lohs mohn-TAHN-tehs ehn lahs PLAH-kahs]
You guys need to nail the studs to the plates.

Necesita clavarlos en los transversales.
[neh-seh-SEE-tah klah-VAHR-lohs ehn lohs trahn-vehr-SAHL-ehs]
You need to nail them onto the crosspieces.

Necesitamos elevar el muro. Cuidado.
[neh-seh-see-TAH-mos eh-leh-VAHR ehl MOO-roh. Kwee-DAH-doh]
We need to raise the wall up. Careful.

Necesitan soportarlo. Bien.
[neh-seh-SEE-tahn soh-por-TAHR-lo. BYEHN-]
You guys need to hold it. Good.

Bueno. Jose, necesita clavarlo.
[MEE-rah. Ho-SAY, neh-seh-SEE-tah klah-VAHR-loh]
O.K. Jose, you need to nail it down.

Necesita traerme un bonche de clavos.
[neh-seh-SEE-tah try-HER-may oon bone-CHEH deh KLAH-vohs]
You need to bring me some (a "bunch" of) nails.

Ojo. Necesitan situar la unión.
[OH-ho. Neh-seh-SEE-tahn seet-oo-AHR lah oo-nee-OHN]
Heads up. You guys need to position the joint (the connection).

For measuring the spacing between studs, one easy method is to cut a fireblock the correct size, and use it as a spacer to position studs top and bottom before nailing each stud to the top and bottom plates. We will get to measurements later, but this will work very well in the meantime. It isn't even a waste of lumber, as you will eventually nail it in place as one of your fireblocks.

STEP THREE — NOUNS

English — Spanish
Notes and Memory Hints

header(s) — **cabezal(es)** *[kah-beh-SAHL-(ehs)]*
Cabeza is the Spanish word for "head" so **cabezal** makes sense for "header". If you blow it and use **cabeza**, you'll still be understood in most cases.

doorway — **portal** *[poor-TAHL]*
Cognate of English word portal—you can also think of a port of any kind as an "opening".

window — **ventana** *[ven-THAN-ah]*
Think "vent" or "ventilation", which most windows provide.

fireblock(s) — **bloque(s) antifuego(s)**
[BLOH-kay(s) ahn-tee-FWAY-goh(s)]

O.K., a bit of a tough one. No problem (I hope) with **bloque**, a cognate of block; **fuego** is Spanish for fire.

side — **lateral** *[lah-tehr-AHL]*

> Easy for you football fans—a lateral is a pitch out to the side, right? That's 'cuz lateral means side. Duh.

post — **poste** *[POHS-teh]*

> An easy cognate. Works for any kind of post—king posts, vertical supports, etc.

ridge board — **tabla de cumbrera**
[TAH-blah de coom-BREHR-ah]
— **transversal** *[trahns-vehr-SAHL]*

> Another tough one. Remember tabla is a word for board (I like to think of a picnic **table**, which is made of boards). Try cumbrera, it's like umbrella, which is like a roof. You can get away with this instead of tabla de cumbrera. Not the "correct" word, but a ridge board is a kind of crosspiece.

rafter — **cabrio** *[KAH-brioh]*

> For you car buffs, a **cabrio** (à la V.W.) is a convertible, which needs "rafters" to keep the soft top up. If you get stuck, use **tabla** or **viga** and point at where it goes. Everyone should get the picture.

eave — **alero** *[ahl-EHR-oh]*

> Hey, I never said they would all be easy. When all else fails, cut and install the first rafter to demo the overhang.

soffit — **sofito** *[soh-FEET-oh]*

> Does anyone out there even know what this sucker is in English? Oh well, at least it's a cognate, for what it's worth.

subroof — *subrufo [soob-ROO-foh]*

> Don't you just love those *Spanglish* words? The

real Spanish word for roof is **techo,** but **rufo** is a whole lot easier.

STEP THREE — VERBS

English — Spanish
Notes and Memory Hints

to level — **nivelar** *[nee-vehl-AHR]*
For those of you who joined us late, we covered this one under foundations. Look there for memory hints.

to square — **cuadrar** *[kwah-DRAHR]*
The **cuad-** part of the word is a cognate with the English quad, as in quadrangle, meaning square.

to hang — **suspender** *[soos-pehn-DEHR]*
"His pants were hanging from his suspenders." Pretty good description of my great-uncle Herman.

TIME TO ROCK AND ROLL AGAIN

Necesita cortar un portal.
[neh-seh-SEE-tah kohr-TAHR oon pohr-TAHL]
You need to cut a doorway.

Necesitamos cortar las ventanas.
[neh-seh-see-TAH-mohs kohr-TAHR lahs vehn-THAN-ahs]
We need to cut out the windows.

Necesitan nivelar los laterales.
[neh-seh-SEE-tahn nee-vehl-AHR lohs lah-tehr-AHL-es]
You guys need to make sure the sides (the upright supports) are level.

Necesitamos poner el cabezal.
[neh-seh-see-TAH-mohs poh-NEHR ehl kah-beh-SAHL]
We need to install the header.

Mire. Necesita cuadrarlo.
[MEER-reh. neh-seh-SEE-tah koo-ahd-RAHR-loh]
Don't forget. You need to square it up.

Necesita suspender las vigas.
[neh-seh-SEE-tah soos-pehn-DEHR lahs VEE-gahs]
You need to hang the ceiling joists.

Necesitan instalar (poner) los postes.
[neh-seh-SEE-tahn eens-TAHL-ar (poh-NEHR) los-POHS-tehs]
You guys need to put up the posts.

Bueno. Necesitamos elevar el transversal.
[BWEHN-oh. neh-seh-see-TAH-mohs ehl-eh-VAHR ehl trahns-vehr-SAHL]
Good. Now we need to lift the ridge board into place.

Necesitan cortar y clavar los cabrios.
[neh-seh-SEE-tahn kohr-TAHR ee klah-VAHR lohs KAHB-ree-ohs]
You guys need to cut and nail in the rafters.

Necesitan poner el subruffo.
[neh-seh-SEE-tahn poh-NEHR ehl soob-RUH-foh]
You guys need to lay the subroof.

Necesitan usar unos-por-cuatros (el triplay).
[neh-seh-SEE-tahn oo-SAHR oo-NOHS por KWAT-rohs. (ehl TREE-plahy)]
Use one-by-fours (plywood).

DO YOU MEASURE UP?

So, knowing how to count in Spanish, you're about halfway to where you need, and probably want, to be with numbers. Working with numbers on the job site normally involves some type of measuring, right? Well, we're here to help.

pulgada(s)
[pool-GAH-dah(s)]

Inch, inches

> Thumb in Spanish is pulgar, so you can probably guess where the word for inch came from. Before there were standardized tape measures and rulers, distances were measured by various body parts.

pie(s)
[PYEH(s)]

Foot, feet

> You guessed it, same as those ugly things dangling at the ends of your legs. Back in the day, the standard measure was the length of the King's foot, which, of course, changed every generation or so. Must have been fun working with building plans.

yarda(s)
[YAHR-dah(s)]

Yard, yards A little bit of *Spanglish*, but almost universally understood and used by native Spanish speakers in the U.S. After all, it's the measuring system we use, so everyone has to learn to adapt to it.

metro
[MEH troh]

Meter or metre

Be careful with this one. If you hear someone using it, find out if they mean yarda or meter. Latin America uses the metric system, and the 3-inch difference between these two measures could cause some headaches.

milla
[MEE-yah]

Mile

Almost a cognate, but watch the pronunciation, especially with the double l, which has an English y sound to it.

cuadrado
[koo-ahd-RAH-doh]

Squared

Cuadro means square, and **cuadrado** literally means squared, as in **dos pulgadas cuadradas** (two square inches), **cinco pies cuadrados** (five square feet), etc.

onza
[OHN-sah]

Ounce

Another cognate, so not too difficult to handle.

libra
[LEE-brah]

Pound

O.K., not everything can be a cognate, but here's a little hint for remembering this one. Ever wonder why the abbreviation for pound is **lb** instead of **pd**? Hello? Try **libra**. Makes a little more sense, doesn't it?

galón
[gah-LOHN]

Gallon   Where we stress the first syllable in English, (GAL-lon), it's the other one that gets the emphasis in Spanish. If you forget and say gallon, you will probably still be understood.

cuarto (de galón)
[KWAHR-toh]

Quart   Word in both languages means a quarter of a gallon. Just add an o onto the English quart, and you'll be close enough. You'll most likely want to add the words de galón when talking about paint or other liquids, because **cuarto** also means room in Spanish. (Hey, a little confusion keeps everyone on their toes, right?)

litro
[LEE-troh]

Liter or litre

Βou will run into this one more than meter, because a lot of liquids in the U.S. are measured in liters these days. Not a big difference—there are 4 quarts, and something like 3.9 liters in a gallon. Nothing to lose any sleep over.

vatio
[BAH-tee-oh]

Watt   We're learning Spanish, but this sounds like watt with a German accent. You know, ve have vays of dealing mit you!

voltio
[VOHL-tee-oh]

Volt   Pretty much a cognate, so I think you can handle this one without a lot of hints or help.

voltaje
[vohl-TAH-heh]

Voltage   So much of a cognate that you could almost
             get by with the English word.

Bonus Word

por
[pohr]

By, per   If any of you have taken Spanish before, you
              will recognize **por** as a Spanish word for "for",
              and you would be right—it does mean that
              sometimes. However, for measurements, a
              two-by-four is a **dos-por-cuatro**; and in vol-
              ume, 10 pounds per square inch is **diez libras
              por pulgada cuadrada.**

ACABADOS

 Yeah, I know—weird word. It comes from the Spanish verb **acabar**, *to finish*. **El acabado** is a general term used for all types of finish work. Before starting this topic, you should go back and review the rough carpentry pages (**freimeando**/framing) to pick up basic vocabulary such as measuring, nailing, drilling, etc. We will not be repeating all that here.

STEP ONE — NOUNS

English — Spanish
Notes and Memory Hints

door — **puerta** *[PWEHR-tah]*
> Sort of like the English portal, which is an entrance, or even port—an entrance to land from the sea.

jamb — **jamba** *[HAHM-bah]*
> Actually a pretty easy cognate, but watch the pronunciation. The letter j in Spanish is pronounced more like our English h.

threshold — **umbral** *[oom-BRAHL]*
> This is one you will have to memorize cold. Doesn't sound like anything in English except umbrella, which ain't even close to the same thing.

header — **dintel** *[DEEN-tehl]*
> Not an easy word to remember. What works for me is to connect it to the English word

lintel, which is the same thing and only one
letter different.

shim — **cuña** [KOON-yah]
> Good all-purpose word to know—used for
> "shim", "wedge", "keystone", etc.

hinge — **bisagra** [bee-SAH-grah]
> Sorry, another tough one. I have no idea
> where the word came from, but it's one you'll
> probably need to memorize.

window — **ventana** [vehn-TAH-nah]
> No easy cognate here. Try thinking of a
> "vent", or "ventilation" which is what windows
> often provide.

glass, pane — **vidrio** [VEE-dree-oh]
       — **cristal** [krees-TAHL]
> For **vidrio**, think vitreous ("glasslike"), as in
> vitreous china sinks and toilets. **Cristal** may
> be easier to remember—quartz crystal is
> clear and was used before glass in windows.

baseboard — **moldura** [mohl-DOO-rah]
> Sounds like "molding", and is actually the
> Spanish word for trim, but should get you by,
> especially with a little pointing. As an added
> bonus, you get to use the same word for door
> and window molding. The Spanish word for
> baseboard, **zócalo**, is not easy to remember.

STEP ONE — VERBS

English — Spanish
> **Notes and Memory Hints**

to "square up" — **cuadrar** [kwahd-RAHR]
> A Quad (that grassy area in the middle of a
> school or office complex) gets its name from
> **cuad-** (the Latin for "square"). Remember:
> quad and **cuad** both mean square.

to level — **nivelar** *[nee-veh-LAHR]*
> Almost a cognate. Try to focus on the "vel" in both words—*le*VEL = ni**VEL**.

to hang — **colgar** *[kohl-GAHR]*
> One that needs to be memorized. If you get stuck and can't remember it, you can always use the old stand-by **instalar**, to install, or even **poner**, to place or put.

to mount — **montar** *[mohn-TAHR]*
> Easy cognate to remember—and kinda flows with the English, like in mounting hinges, cabinet doors, etc. For you cowboys out there, also works for getting on your horse.

to shim — **poner cuñas** *[poh-NEHR KOON-yahs]*
> In Spanish, you don't "shim" something, you "put shims in", instead. Good to know in squaring up door and window frames.

STEP ONE—SHAKE AND BAKE

Necesitamos colgar [poner] las puertas.
[neh-seh-see-TAH-mohs kohl-GAHR (poh-NEHR) lahs poo-EHR-tahs]
We need to hang the doors.

Necesitan instalar las jambas.
[neh-seh-SEE-tahn ehn-stah-LAHR lahs HAHM-bahs]
You guys need to install the door jambs.

Ojo. Necesita cuadrarlo.
[OH-ho. neh-seh-SEE-tah kwahd-RAHR-loh]
Don't forget. You need to square it up.

Necesitamos poner cuñas aquí y aquí.
[neh-seh-see-TAH-mohs poh-NEHR KOON-yahs ah-KEE ee ah-KEE]
We need to shim it here and here.

Ellos necesitan montar las bisagras.
[EH-yohs neh-seh-SEE-tahn mohn-TAHR lahs bees-AHG-rahs]
They need to mount the hinges.

Necesita poner [instalar] las ventanas.
[neh-seh-SEE-tah poh-NEHR (ehn-stah-LAHR lahs vehn-THAN-ahs]
You need to install the windows.

STEP TWO — NOUNS

English — Spanish
 Notes and Memory Hints

staircase — **escalera** *[ehs-kah-LEHR-ah]*
 Not too tough—think escalator, which is
 nothing more than a moving staircase.

stair step or tread
 — **escalón** *[ehs-kah-LOHN]*
 — **peldaño** *[pehl-DAN-yoh]*
 Once you know **escalera**, you can associate
 escalón with it, like staircase and stair in
 English. For **peldaño**, try thinking of a pedal,
 which is something you step on.

banister — **baranda** *[bahr-AHN-dah]*
 Starts with "bar", which is somewhat descrip-
 tive. I always associate "anda" with walking
 (andar=*to walk*), giving me a "walking bar"—a
 banister.

cabinet — **gabinete** *[gah-been-EH-tah]*
 Cognate, but with a g instead of a c. Since
 these two letters sound pretty much alike, if
 you blow it and say **cabinete,** you'll be understood, and it won't be any worse than some of
 the rest of your "gringo" accent.

counter(top) — **tablero** *[tahb-LEHR-oh]*
 — **mostrador** *[mohs-trah-DOHR]*
 If you recall, **tabla** is a word for "board".
 Works for me, as it sounds like table, and a

counter ain't nothing more than another tabletop around my house.

drawer(s) — **cajón(es)** *[kah-HOHN(ehs)]*
Need to memorize, and make sure you get the ah sound right—**cojones** is a whole different subject not covered in this book!

clothes closet
— **ropero** *[roh-PEHR-oh]*
— **armario** *[ahr-MAHR-eh-oh]*
The word for clothes in Spanish is **ropa**, so you hang your **ropa** in the **ropero**. You may also encounter the word **armario**, which is the Spanish equivalent of the fancy French term armoire, generally a freestanding piece of furniture used as a closet.

shelf
— **tabla** *[TAH-blah]*
— **repisa** *[reh-PEES-ah]*
I use **tabla**, because, like **tablero**, it reminds me of table, and like a tabletop, it is a flat surface to put things on. **Repisa** is better Spanish, but it's like I care, y'know?

bracket, support — **soporte** *[soh-POHR-teh]*
There are other words for bracket or brace, but **soporte** is an easy cognate to remember. Can be used for everything from rafter hangers to shelf brackets.

knob
— **pomo** *[POH-moh]*
— **manija** *[mah-NEE-hah]*
No English/Spanish cognate for knob, which came from German. **Manija** is worth memorizing—works for doorknobs and knobs or handles on cabinets and drawers. Comes from the word **mano** = *hand*. As hand is to handle — **mano** is to **manija**.

screw — **tornillo** *[tohr-NEE-yoh]*
Certainly not a cognate, but learnable. Nails

go straight in (hopefully!), while screws turn. *Turn*/**torn-** are cognates, and the **–illo** says it's small (see below), so I remember a screw is "a little thing that turns"—a **tornillo**.

 A little secret to some Spanish suffixes (word endings)—whenever a noun ends in either **ito/ita** or **illo/illa**, it means you are dealing with a small version of whatever it is. A **casa** is a house, so a **casita** is a small house or cottage. A **marro** is a sledge hammer, so a framing hammer is a **martillo**. A **reja** is a grill, making a **rejilla** a small grill such as a wall or ceiling register. From **carreta** for wagon, we get **carretilla** for wheelbarrow, etc. Sounds like useless trivia, but it really does help in understanding and remembering some words.

STEP TWO—VERBS

English — Spanish
>**Notes and Memory Hints**

to support — **soportar** *[soh-pohr-TAHR]*
>Easy cognate which goes with **soporte**, so you get a verb and a noun. One-stop shopping for describing everything from a jockstrap to child-support payments.

to screw — **atornillar** *[tohr-nee-YAHR]*
>O.K., let's keep it clean here. We are talking screwdrivers and little threaded things. If this verb is too much for you, try **usar tornillos** (to use screws).

to put in, insert — **meter** *[meh-TEHR]*
>This has nothing to do with Rosie the Meter Maid. It's what's called a false cognate—looks like the English word meter, but does

70

not mean the same thing. **Instalar, insertar,** and **poner** all work if you draw a blank.

to adjust — **ajustar** *[ah-hoos-TAHR]*
Back to a real cognate you can trust, and trust me, if you learn this verb, you will find a million ways of using it on a job site (to adjust, adapt, fit, tighten, etc.)

to align — **alinear** *[ah-leen-eh-AHR]*
Another easy cognate, which can be used anytime you need to get things like cabinet tops and drawers aligned correctly.

STEP TWO—SHAKE AND BAKE

Necesita instalar [poner] la baranda.
[neh-seh-SEE-tah ehn-stah-LAHR (poh-NEHR) lah bahr-AHN-dah]
You need to install [put in] the banister.

Necesitan poner los gabinetes de cocina.
[neh-seh-SEE-tahn poh-NEHR lohs gah-been-EHT-tehs deh koh-SEEN-ah]
You guys need to put in the kitchen cabinets.

Necesitan montarlos con tornillos.
[neh-seh-SEE-tahn mohn-TAHR-lohs kohn tohr-NEE-yohs]
You guys need to mount them with screws.

Ojo. Necesitamos alinear las tablas.
[OH-ho. neh-seh-see-TAH-mohs ah-leen-eh-AHR lahs TAH-blahs]
Careful. We need to align the countertops.

Ahora necesita meter los cajones.
[ah-OHR-ah neh-seh-SEE-tah may-TEHR lohs kah-HOHN-ehs]
Now you need to insert the drawers.

Mire. Necesita ajustarlos.
[MEER-reh. neh-seh-SEE-tah ah-hoos-TAHR-lohs]
Look here. You need to adjust them.

Y necesita instalar las manijas.
[EE neh-seh-SEE-tah ehn-stah-LAHR lahs mah-NEE-has]
And you need to install the knobs.

Necesita poner una tabla en el ropero.
[neh-seh-SEE-tah poh-NEHR oonah TAH-blah ehn ehl roh-PEHR-oh]
You need to put a shelf in the closet.

Necesita usar los soportes.
[neh-seh-SEE-tah oo-SAHR lohs soh-POHR-tehs]
You need to use the brackets.

YOUR ROOM OR MINE?

Athough some of the vocabulary we are going to give you here can be found in other lessons, we thought it might be a nice idea to give you the whole nine yards in one list. That way, you will have it as a handy reference. You are going to need to know most of these, so the sooner you learn them, the better.

Basic Rooms

livin
[LEE-veen]
sala
[SAH-lah]

Living room   The real Spanish word for this is **la sala**, but the *Spanglish livin* is easy to remember, widely used, and pretty much universally understood among the Spanish-speaking population of the U.S.

comedor
[koh-meh-DOOR]

Dining room   The word for food, especially dinner, is **comida**, and the **comedor** is where you eat it.

cocina
[koh-SEEN-ah]

Kitchen   Tied to the verb **cocinar**, to cook, the **cocina** is the room for cooking.

dormitorio
[dohr-mee-TOHR-ee-oh]

Bedroom   Just think of a dormitory at your local college or university—all those dorm rooms are basically just bedrooms, right? **Dormir** is the verb for to sleep, and **dormitorio** fits right in as the place where you do it.

(cuarto de) baño
[KWAHR-toh deh BAHN-yoh]

Bathroom, bath

Proper Spanish uses the whole **cuarto de baño**, equivalent to our word bathroom, but most people these days just refer to it as the **baño**—the bath, like we do. (At least if you have one. My uncle down in the Ozarks doesn't have 5 rooms and a bath—he's got 4 rooms and a path. Those corncobs really do a number.)

Additional Rooms

salón
[sah-LOHN]

Family room Also sometimes called an **estancia**, but I would recommend **salón** as easier to remember, and it goes with **sala** for the living room next door.

estudio
[ehs-TOO-dee-oh]

Den, study Pretty much a cognate for **study**. Many Spanish cognates of English s words begin with **es**, to pick up the sound of the s in Spanish (remember EHS-seh?).

alacena
[ah-lah-SEH-nah]

Pantry Tough one for beginners. Once you have more vocabulary, you may be able to remember it by linking it to the verb **cenar**—to dine. After

all, you won't be dining very well if the pantry
is bare.

lavandería
[lah-vahn-dehr-EE-ah]

Laundry room

Sometimes called a **cuarto de lavar** (washing
room), but I prefer **lavandería**, because it is
more general. It can mean a laundry room or a
laundramat, so I get two words for the price
of one. Word goes with **lavar**—to wash, and
lavadora—washing machine. If all else fails,
think of Lava soap as a hint.

entrada
[ehn-TRAH-dah]

Entrance, entryway

Just in case you run into one of these that is
separated enough from the living room to be
its own space.

porche
[POHR-cheh]

Porch   Not going to even try to disguise the *Spanglish*
origins of this one. Much easier to remember
than the Spanish words **terraza**—"terrace"
for back porch, and **pórtico** for a front porch.

almacén
[ahl-mah-SEHN]

Storage room

Another of those great, all-purpose words.
An **almacén** can be a storage facility of any
size, from a room to a warehouse—same word
for all.

And, Last But Not Least . . .

75

garage
[gahr-AH-heh]

> I'll let you figure this one out. Pure cognate.

RUFEANDO

STEP ONE — NOUNS

English — Spanish
         Notes and Memory Hints

roof — *rufo* *[ROO-foh]*

        Great *Spanglish* word to use. The proper Spanish word is **techo**, but *rufo*, or even **roof** will be understood by almost everyone.

roof installer — **rufero** *[roo-FEH-roh]*

        Pure *Spanglish*. Words like **rufero** and **rufing** are a lot more common than de proper ones.

subroof — **subruffo** *[soob-ROO-foh]*

        Anyone who can't follow this one? Also called **bajoruffo** ("under-roof").

asphalt — **asfalto** *[ahs-FAHL-toh]*

        Easy cognate to remember. Pronunciation is a little different, but not too hard.

tar — **brea** *[BREH-ah]*

        Either memorize, or use **asfalto** instead. It will probably get you by.

paper — **papel** *[pah-PEHL]*

        Pretty close to a cognate—only one letter difference.

tar paper   — **papel de asfalto** *[pah-PEHL deh ahs-FAHL-toh]*
          — **papel de brea** *[pah-PEHL deh BREH-ah]*

        You can get by with **papel** alone—just point at it. I mean, unless you keep your copy machine or the outhouse on the roof, how many kinds of paper have you got up there?

knife — **naifa** [NAH ee-fah]
> Pure *Spanglish*. Much easier than the Spanish word **cuchillo**, which is hard to remember, and even harder to pronounce.

hammer — **martillo** [mahr-TEE-yoh]
> One you will need to memorize—you'll need it. See Framing for memory hint.

hatchet — **hacha** [AH-chah]
> Because of the blade on a shingling hammer, you may hear workers calling it a **hacha**, which is an easy to remember cognate of hatchet. Pronounced like "gotcha" without the g.

nail(s) — **clavo(s)** [KLAH-vohs]
> No cognate here, but like we said under framing, it is close to "clobber", which is what you are supposed to do with them, anyway.

line — **línea** [LEEN-eh-ah]
> Can be used pretty much wherever you would use line in English. Line as in "row" in Spanish is **hilera**, but **línea** will work and is easier to remember.

STEP ONE — VERBS

English — Spanish
Notes and Memory Hints

to put, to place — **poner** [poh-NEHR]
> No cognate, but at least they both start to put down with "p". Seriously, memorize this one, it has a thousand uses on the job site.

to start — **startear** [stahr-teh-AHR]
> Have I mentioned how much I love these easy *Spanglish* words? Actual Spanish verbs are **empezar** and **comenzar**. Go with what's easy.

to cut — **cortar** *[kohr-TAHR]*
> Almost a cognate. Cut and **cort-** are real close. Many Spanish-speaking workers will even recognize "cut" because the words are so similar.

to nail — **clavar** *[klah-VAHR]*
> Memorize it! Sounds even more like "clobber" than **clavo** does.

to use — **usar** *[oo-SAHR]*
> Easy cognate, but watch the pronunciation— it's oo like in tuna, not the English u, which sounds like the word "you".

to apply — **aplicar** *[ah-plee-KAHR]*
> Another easy cognate which may come in handy from time to time.

STEP ONE — SHAKE AND BAKE

In case you are just joining us for this section, what we are going to do is combine forms of the verb necesitar, which we had you memorize, with some of this vocabulary. Here are some examples of how you can now communicate some important stuff—it may not be pretty, but it will be understood:

Necesitamos poner el rufo.
[neh-seh-see-TAH-mohs poh-NEHR ehl ROO-foh]
We need to put the roof on.

Necesitan startear el rufo.
[neh-seh-SEE-tahn stahr-teh-AHR ehl ROO-foh]
You guys need to start on the roof.

Juan, necesita poner una línea de papel.
[wahn, neh-seh-SEE-tah poh-NEHR OO-nah LEEN-eh-ah deh pah-PEHL]
Juan, you need to roll out (or "put down") a strip of tar paper.

79

Necesita cortarlo.
[neh-seh-SEE-tah kohr-TAHR-loh]
You need to cut it.

Necesita usar la naifa. Con cuidado.
[neh-seh-SEE- tah oo-SAHR lah NAH ee-fah. cohn kwee-DAH-doh]
Use the knife. Be careful.

Bueno. Necesitan clavarlo.
[BWEH-noh. neh-seh-SEE-tahn klah-VAHR-loh]
Good. You guys need to nail it down.

Necesitamos aplicar un poco de asfalto (brea).
[neh-seh-see-TAH-mohs ah-plee-KAHR oon POH-koh deh ahs-FAHL-toh (BREH-ah)]
We need to use a little tar.

Miren. Necesitan poner más papel.
[MEER-ehn. neh-seh-SEE-tahn poh-NEHR mahs pah-PEHL]
Hey. You guys need to put down more paper.

STEP TWO — NOUNS

English — Spanish
Notes and Memory Hints

shingle — **teja** *[TEH-hah]*
> One you have to memorize—not a cognate, doesn't rhyme with anything. Wood shingles are also called **ripias**, which you might be able to remember by using a rip saw to make them.

asphalt shingle — **teja (de asfalto)**
> *[TEH-hah deh ahs-FAHL-toh]*
> If you are only using asphalt shingles, just **teja** will do the trick.

shake — **teja (de madera)** *[TEH-hah deh mah-DEHR-ah]*
> **Madera** is Spanish for wood, remember? Again, if you are only using one roofing material, leave it at **teja**.

roofing tile — **teja** *[TEH-hah]*
> Beginning to sound familiar? Anyone who hasn't got it yet should seriously think about becoming a plumber or something.

chimney — **chimenea** *[cheem-ehn-EH-ah]*
> Such an easy cognate that, if you just say chimney in English, everyone will get it.

vent pipe — **tubo de ventilación**
> *[TOO-boh deh vehn-tee-lah-SYOHN]*
> A mouthful, but logical if you think about it. A pipe is a kind of tube, and ventilación is a cognate. If you can't remember **tubo**, use **pipa** [PEE-pah], which is really a pipe you smoke, but gets used for plumbing as well.

skylight — **tragaluz** *[trah-gah-LOOS]*
> Did I say they would all be easy? It actually makes sense in Spanish—**traga** means to swallow, and **luz** means light. Cool, huh?

flashing — **cubrejuntas** *[koo-breh-HOON-tahs]*
> Another tough one, made up of two words— **cubre** (cover) and **juntas** (joints or unions). In a pinch, you can use the cognate **metal** *[meh-TAHL]*, and point at the flashing.

ladder — **escalera**
> Think "escalator", which takes you up and [ehs-kah-LEHR-ah] down like a ladder. If you know any Spanish, you may know this word as "stairs", and you're right—it means both.

even, equal — **igual** *[ee-GWAHL]*
> Cognate of equal, but means both. Yea, I know this is an adverb, not a noun, but so what, it's a good, very useful word for roofing.

STEP TWO — VERBS

English — Spanish
Notes and Memory Hints

to check — *chequear* [cheh-kee-AHR]
    Pretty obvious, right? Like all *Spanglish* terms,
    it's just the English word used in a Spanish
    format and accent.

to even up — **igualar** *[ee-gwahl-AHR]*
    Like the noun above, this is a cognate of the
    English "to equal". Good one to know.

to place, to position — **situar** *[see-too-AHR]*
    Think "situate". Can be used in place of poner,
    especially when you are trying to get some-
    thing aligned or positioned right.

to bring — **traer** *[trah-EHR]*
    Tough verb, no easy way—you need to memo-
    rize it, because you are going to use it a lot.

STEP TWO — SHAKE AND BAKE

Juan, necesita traerme la escalera.
[wahn, neh-seh-SEE-tah try-EHR-meh lah ehs-kah-LEHR-ah]
Juan, bring me the ladder.

Necesitan startear las tejas.
[neh-seh-SEE-tahn stahr-tee-AHR lahs TEH-hahs]etc.).
You guys need to start the shingles (tiles).

Necesitamos poner una línea de tejas.
[neh-sah-see-TAH-mohs poh-NEHR OO-nah LEEN-eh-ah deh TEH-hahs]
Now we need to put on a row of shingles (shakes, tiles).

Ojo! Necesita chequear y igualarlos.
[OH-hoh. neh-seh-SEE-tah cheh-kee-AHR ee ee-gwah-LAHR-lohs]
Pay attention! You need to check and even them up.

you talking to?" or "who do you mean?"). Likewise, if you used **necesitan**, but it wasn't clear that you meant everyone, the question you will get back would be "**¿quienes?**" ("which ones of us do you mean?").

aquí
[ah-KEE]

Means here, as in "**Necesita ponerlo aquí**" (you need to put it here). Can easily be used by itself, with a little pointing, to get your point across. Goes really well as an answer to "donde?"

allí
[ah-YEE]

Twin to aquí, this one means there. As long as you are learning one, you might as well nail both at once. I personally find it easier to memorize "opposites" together, like **esto/eso** (this/that), and **aquí/allí** (here/there).

y
[ee]

Spanish word for *and*—not a cognate, but so weird as a one-letter word that it is pretty easy to remember. How come I never got spelling tests with gimmies like this?

o
[oh]

Man, if you thought "**y**", was easy, how 'bout "**o**" for or. I mean, it even starts with the same letter. It doesn't get any better than this.

¿por qúe?
[pohr KEH?]

Most of you should have watched enough old
Westerns to know that this means why? in
Spanish. Literally translated, it would be "for
what?", or "what for?", but means why?

porque
[pohr-keh]

You can't have why? without because, and this
is it. Pretty nifty, huh? If you learn how to
ask why, you know how to say because, too.

EXTERIOR

[Once again, before starting this topic, you should go back and review the Foundations and Framing topics, as we are not going to repeat all of the basic vocabulary you learned there, although we will be using some of these words in the example sentences.]

STEP ONE — NOUNS

English — Spanish
 Notes and Memory Hints

framing — **estructura** *[ehs-trook-TOO-rah]*
 Not too tough—just think "structure" to remember this Spanish word for a building's framing.

sheathing — **entablado** *[ehn-tah-BLAH-doh]*
 Tablas are boards, giving us **en-tabla-do** for something **en**closed or covered by boards.

plywood — *triplay [tree-PLAH ee]*
 Spanglish word, variation of the English three-ply with Spanish pronunciation. Much easier than the actual Spanish word **madera prensada**—"pressed wood."

sheathing paper — **papel de entablado**
 [pah-PEL deh ehn-tah-BLAH-doh]
 If you can get entablado, it is pretty easy to add the Spanish cognate for paper, which is papel—only one letter difference. As long as you are dealing with sheathing, just **papel** will probably do fine.

siding — **forrado** *[fohr-AH-doh]*
 Wood or other exterior siding materials are

forrado, which is another one to memorize, as it doesn't sound like anything in English.

STEP ONE — VERBS

English — Spanish
Notes and Memory Hints

to cover — **cubrir** *[koo-BREER]*
Actually a cognate, since b and v sound the same in Spanish. Easy verb to learn and a good one to know.

to wrap — **enrollar** *[ehn-roh-YAHR]*
Cubrir is probably easier to remember, but if you insist on learning the Spanish word "wrapping" instead of "covering", here it is. Be careful—it's a false cognate, which does not mean the same as the English enroll.

to install — **instalar** *[ehn-stah-LAHR]*
An easy cognate—works in most situations where you can't remember poner, for to put in or to place.

STEP ONE — SHAKE AND BAKE

Necesitamos cubrir la estructura.
[neh-seh-see-TAH-mohs koo-BREER lah ehs-trook-TOO-rah]
We need to cover the framing.

Necesitan instalar [poner] el entablado.
[neh-seh-SEE-tahn ehn-stah-LAHR (poh-NEHR) ehl ehn-tah-BLAH-doh]
You guys need to install [put on] the sheathing.

Mire. Necesitan usar el triplay [la madera prensada].
[MEER-eh. neh-seh-SEE-tahn oo-SAHR ehl tree-PLAH-ee (lah mah-DEHR-ah prehn-SAH-dah)]
See—you need to use plywood sheets.

Ahora necesitan cubrirlo con papel.
[ah-OHR-ah neh-seh-SEE-tahn koo-BREER-loh kohn pah-PEL]
Now you guys need to cover it with paper.

Bueno. Necesitamos poner el forrado aquí.
[BWEH-noh. neh-seh-see-TAH-mohs poh-NEHR ehl fohr-RAH-doh ah-KEY]
O.K. We need to put wood siding on here.

STEP TWO — NOUNS

English — Spanish
> **Notes and Memory Hints**

wire backing — **alambre de soporte**
> *[ah-LAHM-breh deh soh-POHR-teh]*
> The tough part here is memorizing the word
> **alambre** for wire. Support/**soporte** are easy
> cognates to remember. Again, just **alambre**
> will get you by—how many other kinds of wire
> could there be for stuccoing?

stucco — **estuco** *[ehs-TOO-koh]*
> There are a couple of other Spanish words
> for this (like **revoque** and **enlucido**), but I
> say, go with the easy cognate.

mixer — **revolvedora** *[reh-vohl-veh-DOOR-ah]*
> Think "to revolve", because that's basically
> what it does. Also called a **mezcladora**, from
> the verb **mezclar**, to mix.

wheelbarrow — **carrilla** *[kahr-REE-yah]*
> — **carretilla** *[kahr-reh-TEE-yah]*
> The **carr-** sound is like "cart", which it is. The
> **-illa** tells you it is smaller than a donkey cart
> (see the worried gringo guide in the **Acabado**
> topic for a fuller explanation).

trowel — **llana** *[YAH-nah]*
> No cognate here, but it's the English word
> that's the weird one. **Llana** comes from the
> verb **allanar**, to smooth, and the noun **llano**,

which means smooth. See the musical memory
hint in the section on foundations.

STEP TWO — VERBS

English — Spanish
Notes and Memory Hints

to mix — **mezclar** *[mehs-KLAHR]*
Pretty close to a cognate, so it shouldn't be
hard to memorize and use. Even if you get
confused and say "**mix-clar**", you will be
understood—it's close enough.

to dump
— *dompear[dohm-peh-AHR]*
— **descargar***[dehs-kahr-GAHR]*
Use the *Spanglish* and you'll be understood. But
if you prefer, **descargar** is another cognate
for the English word "discharge".

to pour — **vaciar** *[vah-SYAHR]*
Memorizing a few won't hurt.

to trowel, to smooth — **allanar** *[ah-YAHN-ahr]*
Goes with **llana** (trowel), and **llano** (smooth)
If it is one you need to know, memorize it,
otherwise don't put yourself out.

STEP TWO — SHAKE AND BAKE

Necesita clavar el alambre (de soporte).
[neh-seh-SEE-tah klah-VAHR ehl ah-LAHM-breh deh soh-POHR-the]
You need to nail on the wire (backing).

Necesitamos mezclar el estuco.
[heh-say-see-TAH-mohs mehs-KLAHR ehl esh-TOO-koh]
We need to mix some stucco.

Necesita *dompearlo* **en la carrilla.**
[neh-seh-SEE-tah dohm-peh-AHR-lo ehn lah kahr-REE-yah]
You need to dump (pour) it in the wheelbarrow.

Necesitan poner el estuco en los muros.
[neh-seh-SEE-tahn poh-NEHR ehl ehs-TOO-koh ehn lohs MOO-rohs]
You guys need to stucco the walls.

Mire. Necesita allanarlo.
[MEER-eh. neh-seh-SEE-tah ah-yah-NAHR-loh]
Watch. You need to trowel (smooth) it.

Ojo. Necesita mojarlo más.
[OH-ho. neh-seh-SEE-tah moh-HAHR-loh mahs]
Watch it. You need to wet it more.

HOW 'BOUT A DATE?

At some point, and probably sooner than later, you are going to need to communicate something about some day or month other than the present, right? I mean, how else are you going to talk about work schedules, days off, paydays, your birthday (who knows, somebody might like you enough to buy you a new nail punch or something), or when the next job is due to start. The days of the week in Spanish will require some straight memorization, but the months are pretty much a no-brainer.

Days of the Week

Sunday — **Domingo** *[doh-MEEN-goh]*
> Not even close to a cognate. Comes from the Latin *domini* for God, which matches up pretty good with our current concept of Sunday, as opposed to the original German mythological concept of Sun-day.

Monday — **Lunes** *[LOO-nehs]*
> The mythological origin of our word was Moon-day, which is actually consistent with the Spanish, since **luna** is the Spanish word for moon. (We get words like lunar from the same Latin source.)

Tuesday — **Martes** *[MAHR-tehs]*
> What can I say? If you like Mardi Gras, you might be you might be interested in knowing that it is French for Fat Tuesday. O.K., probably not, but Mardi in French is the same as **Martes** in its sister language, Spanish, and they both mean Tuesday.

Wednesday — **Miércoles** *[mee-EHR-koh-lehs]*
> One you just have to memorize cold—weird in

95

both languages. Miércoles doesn't sound like or rhyme with anything in English, so you're on your own here.

Thursday — **Jueves** *[WHOEH-vehs]*

Try something like "I always buy eggs (**huevos**) on Thursday (**Jueves**)." Hey, I'm trying here—any port in a storm. The sounds are similar, so give it a try.

Friday — **Viernes** *[VYEHR-nehs]*

Trust me, you will learn and remember this one. TGIF is just as important a concept in Spanish as in English. Everyone waits for Friday to get here.

Saturday — **Sábado** *[SAH-bah-doh]*

Not too different, and even easier to remember if you think Sabbath day, which actually is Saturday, not Sunday.

Months of the Year

As I promised you, these are much easier—January is the only one you really have to work at. The rest just require some slight changes in pronunciation.

January — **enero** *[ehn-EHR-oh]*
February — **febrero** *[feh-BREH-roh]*
March — **marzo** *[MAHR-soh]*
April — **abril** *[ah-BREEL]*
May — **mayo** *[MAH-yoh]*
June — **junio** *[WHO-nee-oh]*
July — **julio** *[WHO-lee-oh]*
August — **agosto** *[ah-GOHS-toh]*
September — **septiembre** *[sehp-TYEHM-breh]*
October — **octubre** *[ohk-TOO-breh]*
November — **noviembre** *[noh-VYEHM-breh]*
December — **diciembre** *[dee-SYEHM-breh]*

That's all there is to it. Combine these with your numbers, and you can say any date you want in Spanish.

Friday, July thirty-first.
Viernes, treinta y uno de julio.

Monday, September third.
Lunes, tres de septiembre.

Wednesday, March fifteenth.
Miércoles, quince de marzo.

Lesson 7: Sheetrocking

SHIROQUEANDO

STEP ONE — NOUNS

English — Spanish
Notes and Memory Hints

sheetrock — *shiroque* *[shee-ROH-keh]*
> *Spanglish* word which tries to pick up the sound of "sheetrock" in English.

sheetrock installer — *shiroquero* *[shee-roh-KEH-roh]*
> A related *Spanglish* term. The "ero" at the end means a guy who does that kind of work: carpintero, plomero, rufero, etc.

knife — *naifa* *[NAH ee-fah]*
> O.K., while we're tossing out *Spanglish* words, here is another great one. Much easier than the Spanish word **cuchillo** for knife.

hammer — **martillo** *[mahr-TEE-yoh]*
> The "illo" ending in Spanish means a little one. So, name your hammer "Little Marty," and you will remember **martillo**.

nail(s) — **clavo(s)** *[KLAH-voh(s)]*
> In case you just joined us, it sounds a little like "clobber", which is what you're supposed to do to them.

screw(s) — **tornillo(s)** *[tohr-NEE-yoh(s)]*
> Sounds like "turn", or maybe attorney—some people think they specialize in screwing people. O.K., now we are probably going to get screwed—I mean, sued.

stud — **montante** *[mohn-THAN-the]*
> See memory hint in framing section.

STEP ONE — VERBS

to measure — **medir** [meh-DEER]
> Once again, memorize the rule (which you
> must have if you've been reading this book)
> "You must always measure, m'dear", and you
> will remember this one.

to cut — **cortar** [kohr-TAHR]
> As said before, almost a cognate—cut and
> **cort-** are pretty close. The beauty of cog-
> nates is that they work both ways.

to install — **instalar** [eehn-stah-LAHR]
> Easy Spanish cognate—pronounced pretty
> much like the English.

to nail — **clavar** [klah-VAHR]
> Goes with clavo, and sounds even more like
> "clobber". Learn it already. Nothing more
> basic than hammers and nails (unless you're a
> plumber or bricklayer).

STEP ONE — SHAKE AND BAKE

One more time, for any of you shiroqueros who skipped all
the previous sections, what we do here is combine forms
of the verb necesitar which you just memorized (you did
memorize it, didn't you?) with this new vocabulary, to see
what we can communicate:

Necesitamos poner (install) el shiroque.
[neh-seh-see-TAH-mohs poh-NEHR (ehn-stah-LAHR) ehl shee-ROH-keh]
*We need to put up (install) the sheetrock (the plaster-
board).*

Pedro, necesita medir y cortarlo.
[PEH-droh, neh-seh-SEE-tah meh-DEER ee kohr-TAHR-loh]
Pedro, you need to measure and cut it.

Miren. Necesitan clavarlo a los montantes.
[MEER-ehn. neh-seh-SEE-tahn klah-VAHR-lo ah lohs mohn- TAHN-tehs]
O.K. You guys need to nail it to the studs.

Ojo. Necesita levantarlo (bajarlo) un poco.
[OH-ho. neh-seh-SEE-tah leh-vahn-TAHR-loh (bah-HAR-loh) oon POH-koh]
Watch it. You need to raise it (lower it) a little.

Bueno. Necesita poner los tornillos.
[BWEHN-oh. neh-seh-SEE-tah poh-NEHR lohs tohr-NEE-yohs]
Good. Now put in the screws.

STEP TWO — NOUNS

wall   — **muro** *[MOO-roh]*
         — **pared** *[pah-REHD]*
         Think "mural"—a painting on a wall. **Pared** is a little tougher. Probably just have to memorize it, or stick with muro.

joint — **unión** *[oo-neh-OHN]*
         I know this is a bad word for some of you in Dixie, but a union is a joint or connection.

tape — *teip [teh -eep] Heck, just say it in English!*
         Another useful *Spanglish* word. Excellent cognate!

taping compound — **pasta de muro** *[PAHS-tah deh MOO-roh]*
         You can get by with just **pasta**, which is a cognate of "paste"— ever overcook a pot of pasta? What you get is pretty much white, sticky paste, right?

plaster — **yeso** *[YEH-soh]*
         One to memorize. Workers will call taping compound **yeso** sometimes, as it looks and mixes a lot like plaster.

taping trowel — **paleta** *[pah-LEH-tah]*
         Only makes sense if you're an artist who uses

a pallet—looks like a putty knife, used for smearing oil paint on canvas.

coat — **capa** *[KAH-pah]*
Think "cap", or "cape", both of which are covers or "coats".

sandpaper — **lija** *[LEE-hah]*
O.K., help me out here. I have no clue except to memorize it.

STEP TWO — VERBS

to apply — **aplicar** *[ah-plee-KAHR]*
Pretty close to a cognate. Think applicant, which is what you are if you apply for a job. **Aplicar**/applicant sound almost the same.

to tape — *teipear* *[tey-PEAHR]*
Can we all say *Spanglish,* amigos? One I don't expect you to forget—it's a natural.

to smooth — **alisar** *[ah-lees-AHR]*
Lisa in Spanish means "flat"—and you can all get your minds out of the gutter. This is not a description of anyone named Lisa.

to sand — **lijar** *[lee-HAHR]*
Goes with **lija** for sandpaper. No hints here—one you'll have to memorize.

to clean — **limpiar** *[leem-pee-AHR]*
No "limp" wrist here—you have to scrub to get it clean.

STEP TWO — SHAKE AND BAKE

Necesitamos *teipear* **los muros.**
[neh-seh-see-TAH-mohs tey-PEAHR lohs MOO-rohs]
We need to tape the walls.

102

Necesitan aplicar pasta en las uniones y clavos.
[neh-seh-SEE-tahn ahp-lee-KAHR PAHS-tah ehn lahs oon-eh-OHN-ehs ee
KLAH-vohs]
*You guys need to spread taping compound on the joints and
nails.*

Bueno. Necesitan aplicar *teip***, y más pasta (yeso).**
[BWEH-noh. neh-seh-SEE-tahn ah-plee-KAHR TEH eep ee mahs PAHS-tah
(YEH-soh]
*Good. Now add the tape, and more taping compound (plas-
ter).*

Mire. Necesita usar la paleta y alisarlo.
[MEER-eh. neh-seh-SEE-tah oo-SAHR lah pah-LEH-tah ee ah-lee-SAHR-
loh]
Watch. You need to smooth it out with a taping trowel.

Necesitan lijar la pasta (lijarlo).
[neh-seh-SEE-tahn lee-HAHR lah PAHS-tah (lee-HAHR-loh)]
You guys need to sand the compound (or, sand it).

Ojo. Necesitamos limpiar los muros (las paredes).
[OH-ho. neh-seh-see-TAH-mohs leem-pee-AHR lohs MOO-rohs (lahs pah-
REHD-ehs]
Heads up. We need to clean the walls.

IF YOU'VE GOT THE MONEY, HONEY, I'VE GOT THE TIME . . .

Let's first look at some words related to time:

¿cuándo? *[KWAHN-doh]*

> Means *when?* Really handy to recognize as you are giving someone instructions to do something. Pretty typical for the person to ask "when?"

ahora *[ah-OHR-ah]*

> *Now.* Memorize this one quickly, because you are going to be using it a lot. Actually, we can kill two birds with one stone here, because **hora** means *hour* in Spanish. **Ahora** literally means *at this hour* which equals *now*.

ahorita *[ah-ohr-EE-tah]*

> If you want to put a little more sense of urgency in it, use **ahorita!** instead—means **right now.** But be aware that if it comes in an answer, it means *in a moment* or *later.*

ahora mismo! *[ah-OHR-ah MEES-moh]*

ahorita mismo! *[ah-ohr-EE-tah MEES-moh]*

> Both mean Right Now!! So to add extra urgency add **mismo** if you really mean it.

en un momento *[ehn OON moh-MEN toh]*

> In a moment. This literal translation works well in Spanish.

después *[dehs- POOEHS]*

> By itself means *later* — **después de** means after, as in **después de**. . . doing something, do something else.

105

dentro de poco *[DEHN-troh deh POH-koh]*

In a little while—literally, "within a little bit".
Using this expression will really impress your
Spanish-speaking friends.

hoy *[oy]*

Spanish word for today. Not a cognate, but
not too hard to remember—remember that
the h is silent, so it sounds *oy* as in *oy vey!*

mañana *[mahn-YAH-nah]*

I'm gonna guess that most of you know this
means tomorrow. Also means morning in
expressions like **en la mañana** ("in the morning", not "in the tomorrow").

ayer *[ah-YEHR]*

Yesterday. By learning yesterday, today and
tomorrow, you take care of most immediate
business.

tarde *[TAHR-deh]*

This means both afternoon and late. Makes
sense to me—**tarde** is a cognate of the
English tardy, which means late. And in most
of our lines of work, if someone doesn't show
up until afternoon, he is definitely late,
right?

temprano *[tehm-PRAH-noh]*

As long as we gave you **tarde**, you might as
well learn his twin brother, **temprano**, which
means early. This is another pair which should
be memorized together—**temprano/tarde**.
Add **más** before temprano or tarde to make
them **más temprano** = *earlier* or **más tarde** =
later.

noche *[NOH-cheh]*

Means night in Spanish—please don't confuse
with **nachos**, which the roach coach offers,
but doesn't have anything to do with **noche**.

por la mañana *[pohr lah mahn-YAH-nah]*

> *In the morning*, as in **mañana por la mañana**
> (tomorrow morning). It is also common to use
> **mañana en la mañana**" (tomorrow **in** the
> morning). If that is easier to remember, go
> for it.

por la tarde *[pohr lah TAHR-deh]*

> *Afternoon, in the afternoon*. Works the same
> as above. If you said hoy **en** la tarde instead
> of hoy **por** la tarde, everyone will know you
> mean "this afternoon".

por la noche *[pohr lah NOH-cheh]*

> *At night*. Same-o, same-o. Ditto. See above.

Remember that most of the Quickies in this book give you
the ability to communicate easily, without getting hung up
on putting together complete sentences. When someone
asks you, "cuándo?" you can give short, perfectly understandable answers, like **"ahora"**, **"mañana"**, **"hoy por** [or **en**]
la tarde", **"en un momento"**, **"dentro de poco"**, etc.

ELÉCTRICO

STEP ONE — NOUNS

English — Spanish
Notes and Memory Hints

electrician — **electricista** *[eh-lehk-tree-SEE-stah]*
May be a cognate, but a bit of a tongue twister to pronounce.

electricity — **electricidad** *[eh-lehk-tree-SEE-dahd]*
The secret here is to remember that words like this ending in *ty* in English all end in **dad** in Spanish (*variety*/**variedad**, *simplicity*/**simplicidad**, etc.).

wall — **muro** *[MOO-roh]*
— **pared** *[pah-REHD]*
Think "mural", which is a painting on a wall. Don't know what to tell you on **pared**. Either memorize it, or use **muro**.

stud — **montante** *[mohn-THAN-teh]*
Covered brilliantly under framing. Enough said.

conduit — **conducto** *[kohn-DOOK-toh]*
Not quite a cognate, but close. The conduit conducts the wires to the right locations.

electrical receptacle — **caja** *[KAH-hah]*
Actually, **caja** means "box", any kind of box—toolbox, receptacle, coffin, whatever. Save yourself some grief and learn **caja**. It'll get you by.

fitting, connection — **conexión** *[kohn-ehx-SYON]*
Pretty easy cognate to learn and remember. Can be used for any kind of connection.

drill — **taladro** *[tah-LAH-droh]*
> You'll have to memorize it cold—doesn't sound like anything in English. However, see the shortcut box below.

hammer — **martillo** *[mahr-TEE-yoh]*
> Learn it. Things don't get much more basic than hammers and nails, so you'll need to memorize.

nail(s) — **clavo(s)** *[KLAH-voh(s)]*
> As I've said before, sounds a little like "clobber", which is what you do to them.

STEP ONE — VERBS

English — Spanish
Notes and Memory Hints

to drill — **taladrar** *[tah-lahd-RAHR]*
> This is a tough one—doesn't sound like anything in English. However, see notes in shortcut box below.

to put, to place — **poner** *[poh-NEHR]*
> Not much possibility here, except they all start with p. This is a really important verb to memorize, as you will use it a lot.

to push — *puchar* *[poosh-AHR]*
> Easy *Spanglish* word which imitates the English sound "push". Much easier to remember than the Spanish verb for it, which is empujar.

to pull — **jalar** *[hah-LAHR]*
> Think "to haul", which is a form of pulling, for a good word association.

to nail — **clavar** *[klah-VAHR]*
> Sounds even more like "clobber" than clavo does. When you need to drive nails, think about clobbering those suckers.

110

to connect — **conectar** *[koh-nekt-AHR]*

> Easy cognate to learn. Even the pronunciation isn't too different—just saying the English "connect" with an -ar on the end will get you real close.

One of the nice things about the use of *Spanglish* is that, besides making new "Spanish" words out of English words, people often just use the English word itself in the middle of a sentence. The word drill is a whole lot easier than **taladrar**, and will probably be recognized by many Spanish-speaking workers. If not, try to demo what you want a few times, using the word drill, until everyone gets it. Pretty soon, everyone will be using the drill, and you can take your time learning **taladrar**.

STEP ONE — SHAKE AND BAKE

This is where we take the forms of the verb necesitar, which you have memorized, and combine them with these new words, to show how it is possible to communicate on the job. These are just a few of the combinations you can make:

Necesitan instalar las cajas.
[neh-seh-SEE-tahn een-stahl-AHR lahs KAH-hahs]
You guys need to install the receptacles.

Mire. Necesitan clavarlos a los montantes.
[MEER-ah. neh-seh-SEE-tahn klah-VAHR-lohs ah lohs mohn-THAN-tehs]
See. You need to nail them to the studs.

Necesitamos poner los conductos.
[neh-seh-see-TAH-mohs poh-NEHR lohs kohn-DOOK-tohs]
We need to put in all the conduit.

Juan, necesita taladrar (or "drill") los montantes.
[wahn, neh-seh-SEE-tah tah-lahd-RAHR lohs mohn-THAN-tehs]
Juan, you need to drill the studs.

Necesitan *puchar* **el conducto.**
[neh-seh-SEE-tahn poosh-AHR ehl kohn-DOOK-toh]
You guys need to push the conduit (through the studs).

Necesita jalarlo, Pedro.
[neh-seh-SEE-tah hah-LAHR-loh, PEH-droh]
You need to pull it, Pedro.

Bueno. Necesitamos conectarlo a las cajas.
[BWEH-noh. neh-seh-see-TAH-mohs koh-nekt-AHR-loh ah lahs Kah-hahs]
Good. Now we need to connect it to the receptacles.

STEP TWO — NOUNS

English — Spanish
Notes and Memory Hints

wire   — **alambre** *[ahl-AHM-breh]*
          — **cable** *[KAH-bleh]*
          Alambre is the main word for wire, and you'll
          just have to memorize it. In a pinch, you can
          get by with cable, which is a pretty obvious
          cognate of cable, but watch the pronuncia-
          tion—it's tricky.

ground — **cable a tierra** *[KAH-bleh ah tee-EHR-ah]*
          Tierra is Spanish for ground or "earth", mak-
          ing this your ground cable or wire.

outlet — *ploga* *[PLOH-gah]*
          Great *Spanglish* word for English "plug". The
          actual Spanish word is enchufe, which is
          handy to know, but ploga is a lot easier.

switch — *suiche* *[SWEE-cheh]*
          Spanglish sure do make life easier. The actual
          Spanish word interruptor ("interrupter")

112

does make sense, but suiche is a whole lot easier to remember.

circuit — **circuito** *[seer-KEE-toh]*

As long as we are on the subject, here is an easy cognate for you.

circuit breaker — *suiche* **de circuito**
[SWEE-cheh deh seer-KEE-toh]
— **interruptor de circuito**
[een-tehr-oop-TOHR deh seer-KEE-toh]
Now that you know suiche and circuito, is there anyone who can't follow this one? I think I can trust you all here.

breaker panel

— **caja principal** *[KAH-hah preen-see-PAHL]*
— **panel principal** *[PAHN-ehl preen-see-PAHL]*
Principal is a cognate of principal, which means "main". Think of a school principal as being the "main man" (at least mine was--dude swung a mean paddle!).

fuse box — **caja de fusibles** *[KAH-hah deh foos-EE-blehs]*
Just in case you run into one of these in a remodel, fusible(s) is almost a cognate of fuse(s).

fixture(s) — **accesorio(s)** *[ah-sehs-OHR-ee-oh(s)]*
Pretty obvious cognate of accessory. **Luz** is Spanish for light, so lighting fixtures are **accesorios de luz**.

outlet cover(s), switch plate(s) — **placa(s)** *[PLAH-kah(s)]*
Good general word for plates of all kinds around the job site. Think of a "plaque", which is something you attach to the wall. (Yeah, it grows on your teeth, too, but what's that got to do with anything, Sherlock?)

113

STEP TWO — VERBS

English — Spanish
   Notes and Memory Hints

to bend, to fold — **doblar** *[doh-BLAHR]*
   Think to "double", "double back", "double over" as a way of bending or folding things.

to attach   — **conectar** *[koh-nekt-AHR]*
      — **unir** *[oon-EER]*
   Two good cognates: *connect*/**conectar** and *unite*/**unir**. Both will work well for attaching things, so take your pick.

to flip (a switch) — *flipear [flee-pee-AHR]*
   Another handy *Spanglish* verb. Also means to "flip out", but hopefully you won't have anyone go postal on you.

to turn on — **encender** *[ehn-sehn-DEHR]*
   Even with *flipear*, this is not a bad one to memorize. There are times when you may want to be specific about on/off, and not just say "flip the switch, dude."

to turn off — **apagar** *[ah-pah-GAHR]*
   Same as above—**apagar** is the only real word for turning off electrical switches/appliances. In a pinch, you could get by with **cortar**, the verb for "to cut" or "to cut off".

STEP TWO — SHAKE AND BAKE

O.K. Necesitamos jalar el alambre (el cable).
[O.K. neh-seh-see-TAH-mohs hah-LAHR ehl ahl-AHM-breh ehl KAH-bleh]
O.K. We need to pull the wire.

Necesitan cortarlos.
[neh-seh-SEE-tahn kohr-TAHR-lohs]
You guys need to cut them.

Bueno. Necesita conectarlos a los *suiches* (*plogas*, **interruptores de circuito, etc.)**
[BWEH-noh. neh-seh-SEE-tah koh-nekt-AHR-lohs ah lohs SWEE-chehs (PLOH-gahs, een-tehr-oop-TOHR-ehs deh SEER-kee-tohs)]
Good. Now attach them to the switches (outlets, circuit breakers, etc.).

Necesito instalar los accesorios de luz.
[neh-seh-SEE-toh een-stah-LAHR lohs ack-seh-SOH-ryohs deh loos]
I need to install the light fixtures.

Necesita poner las placas.
[neh-seh-SEE-tah poh-NEHR lahs PLAH-kahs]
You need to put on the switch plates and outlet covers.

Juan, necesita *flipear* **el** *suiche*.
[HWAHN, neh-seh-SEE-tah flee-pee-AHR ehl SWEE-cheh]
Juan, flip the switch.

Ojo. Necesita apagar el *suiche* **de circuito.**
[OH-ho. nay-sy-SEE-tah ah-pah-GAHR ehl SWEE-cheh deh SEER-kwee-toh]
Don't forget to turn off the breaker switch.

BONUS WORDS — COLORS

Since wire coloring can be just a little bit important in your line of work, we thought we would throw in a few of the colors you will need to know:

English — Spanish
Notes and Memory Hints

white — **blanco** [BLAHN-koh]
Think "blank", like a blank sheet of paper is nothing but white staring back at you.

black — **negro** [NEH-groh]
Be careful with the pronunciation here.
Learn to say it right, as the English pronunciation will not be understood.

115

green — **verde** *[VEHR-deh]*
> One you'll have to memorize. It doesn't sound much like green, which comes from the German grün. (Like you care, but hey! nothing wrong with learning a bit of German too!)

red — **rojo** *[ROH-hoh]*
> A little better—at least it starts with r, just like red does. Important to learn.

PLOMERIA

STEP ONE — NOUNS

English — Spanish
Notes and Memory Hints

piping — **tubería** [too-beh-REE-ah]
— **cañería** [kah-nyeh-REE-ah]
> Just think of piping as "tubing" and you've got it. Also called **cañería** (the natives used bamboo and other hollow cane plants as pipes).

pipe — **tubo** [TOO-boh]
— *pipa* [PEE-pah]
> See above—a pipe is a "tube" (**tubo**) or a **caño**. In a pinch, you can call it a **pipa**, which is really the word for a pipe you smoke, but does get used as a *Spanglish* word for plumbing pipe.

fitting — **conexión** [koh-nex-SYON]
> *Connection*/**conexión** is a handy cognate. **Conexión** can be used for fitting, junction, union, etc.

T (fitting) — **conexión en T** [koh-nex-SYON ehn teh]
> Once you get the hang of the pronunciation it's just like the English—a T is a T in both languages.

L or "elbow" — **conexión en L** [koh-nex-SYON ehn EH-leh]
— **codo** [KOH-doh]
> Same thing here—just the pronunciation is different. Often referred to as **codo**, which is the Spanish word for elbow.

coupling — **copla** *[KOH-plah]*
>   Pretty close to a cognate, but watch the pro-
>   nunciation—it's *kohp-*, not *kup-*.

drain — **drenaje** *[drehn-AH-heh]*
>   — **desagüe** *[deh-SAH-gweh]*
>   Use **drenaje**, which is closer to English
>   "drain" and "drainage" and much easier to
>   remember.

wrench — **llave** *[YAH-veh]*
>   No easy cognate here—one you just have to
>   memorize. A pipe wrench is actually a **llave
>   francesa** ("French wrench")—how very
>   poetic!

Maybe you learned **llave** as the Spanish word for key instead of wrench.
Truth is, it means both. When you
think about it, this actually makes its
own kind of perverted sense. A key
and a wrench are both essentially
tools inserted to open/loosen or
close/tighten something. Any kind of
wrench used to open and close a valve
or a water main is often referred to as a key in English.

STEP ONE — VERBS

English — Spanish
>   **Notes and Memory Hints**

to put (in), to place — **poner** *[poh-NEHR]*
>   Not much possibility here, except they all
>   start with p. This is a really important verb
>   to memorize—you're going to need it.

to install — **instalar** *[een-stah-LAHR]*
>   Easy cognate to remember. Can be used in
>   place of poner, depending on what you are
>   trying to say.

to use — **usar** [oo-SAHR]

> Real handy cognate to learn, because it has so many uses (where do I get these?). Seriously, it's hard to tell someone which parts or tools to use without knowing this verb.

to tighten — **apretar** [ah-preh-TAHR]

> When you tighten a fixture, you better "pray" you don't strip the threads. You can get by with **instalar** if you draw a blank on **apretar**.

to remove — **remover** [reh-moh-VEHR]

> Another easy cognate which is handy to know. See below.

to loosen — **aflojar** [ah-floh-HAHR]

> When you loosen a valve, you open up the "flow". Ya, I know that's pretty weak, but hey, I'm trying here. In a pinch, you can always use **remover**.

STEP ONE — SHAKE AND BAKE

Necesita/necesitan instalar (poner) la tubería.
[neh-seh-SEE-tah/neh-seh-SEE-tahn ehn-stah-LAHR la too-behr-EE-ah]
You/you guys need to install the plumbing.

Necesitamos instalar los tubos en la cocina.
[neh-seh-see-TAH-mos ehn-stah-LAHR lohs TOO-bohs ehn la koh-SEEN-ah]
We need to install the pipes in the kitchen

Necesitan ponerlos en los baños.
[neh-seh-SEE-tahn poh-NEHR-lohs ehn lohs BAHN-yohs]
You guys need to put them in the baths.

Necesita usar un codo (una copla) aquí.
[neh-seh-SEE-tah oos-AHR oon KOH-doh (oona KOHP-lah) ah-KEY]
Look—you need to use an elbow (a coupling) here.

Atención. Necesitan apretarlos.
[Ah-tehn-SYON. neh-seh-SEE-tahn ah-preh-TAHR-lohs]
Don't forget to tighten them, you guys.

Necesita usar la llave grande aquí.
[neh-seh-SEE-tah oo-SAHR la YAH-veh GRAHN-deh ah-KEY]
You need to use the big wrench here.

Cuidado. Necesita aflojarlo un poco.
[kwee-DAH-doh. neh-seh-SEE-tah ahf-loh-HAHR-loh oon POH-koh]
Careful. You need to loosen it a little.

STEP TWO — NOUNS

English — Spanish
      Notes and Memory Hints

bathtub — **bañera** *[bahn-YEHR-ah]*
> **Baño** is *bath,* making something you take a
> bath in a **bañera**. A *bathroom* is a **cuarto de
> baño**—a room for the bath, but is frequently
> just called **el baño**—*the bath.*

shower stall — **ducha** *[DOO-chah]*
> I know I'm in trouble here, 'cuz this sounds
> like douche in English. Acutally, they both
> come from the same Latin origin, which means
> a jet spray of water directed at the body (or
> at least some part of the body).

toilet
> 1. **inodoro** *[een-oh-DOH-roh]*
> This is where the "odor" goes "in". A com-
> monly used Spanish word for toilet.
>
> 2. **excusado** *[ehs-koo-SAH-doh]*
> Some of you definitely need to say "excuse
> me" a few times when using one of these.
>
> 3. **retrete** *[reh-TREH-teh]*
> Do you use the throne as your private
> "retreat" to catch up on some reading?

4. sanitario *[sah-nee-TAHR-ee-oh}*
A whole lot more "sanitary" than having to dig your own hole every time.

**5. *toilet* *[same as English]*
Use this *Spanglish* term as first choice. But you need to know the others too for an emergency!

sink — *sink [seenk]*

Spanglish, as you might have guessed. Actual Spanish word is **lavabo**, which is from the verb **lavar**, to wash. Think lavatory, which is what ol' Miss Battleaxe made you call the bathroom in the third grade every time you raised your hand 'cuz you really had to "go", remember?

fixture(s) — **accesorio(s)** *[ack-seh-SOH-ryoh(s)]*
— **artefacto(s)** *[ahr-teh-FAHK-toh(s)]*
A cognate for *accessories* in English. Easier to remember than artefactos.

plug, stopper — *ploga [PLOH-gah]*
Another *Spanglish* word, easier than the Spanish word **tapón**, which looks like tampon, and for obvious reasons (same Latin origin).

faucet — **grifo** *[GREE-foh]*
Not much help here—unless you can think "grip", which is what you have to do to turn it on.

mixing valve — **llave de mezcla** *[YAH-veh deh MEHS-klah]*
Llave, which you already know, means wrench and key, is also used for faucet (which is its own kind of key or wrench to turn the water on and off). **Mezclar** is the Spanish verb for "to mix", so the two together give us what we want.

trap — **trampa** *[TRAHM-pah]*
> Almost a cognate, just remember to throw in the letter m.

drain — **drenaje** *[drehn-AH-heh]*
> Again, close to a cognate, but not quite. **Desagüe** also means drain in Spanish, but **drenaje** is closer to the English, and easier to remember.

dishwasher — **lavaplatos** *[lah-vah-PLAH-tohs]*
> From **lavar**, to wash, and **platos**, dishes. Makes just as much sense as the English.

washing machine — **lavadora** *[lah-vah-DOOR-ah]*
> Also from **lavar**, means a "machine that washes". A drier is a **secadora**, from **secar**, to dry.

STEP TWO — VERBS

English — Spanish
> **Notes and Memory Hints**

to join, connect — **unir** *[oo-NEER]*
> Same as English, "to unite". Can be used when you can't remember **conectar**. The noun form is unión, for a joint or union.

to thread (pipe) — **roscar** *[rohs-KAHR]*
> Sorry, no cognates for this one. You might try thinking of all those thread cuts as "rows of scars" on the pipe.

to drill — **taladrar** *[tah-lahd-RAHR]*
> Another tough one—no way out of this one except to memorize it, or grab a drill and demonstrate what you want done.

to measure — **medir** *[meh-DEER]*
> Memorize the little saying, "You must always measure, m'dear", and you will remember that

measure = **medir**. Did I mention this one before? I thought so.

to bend — **doblar** [doh-BLAHR]
Think "to double over", which requires bending.

to cut — **cortar** [kohr-TAHR]
Pretty close to a cognate—cut and **cort-** are very similar.

to position — **situar** [see-too-AHR]
"To situate", which some of you may use already in English for positioning various things.

STEP TWO — SHAKE AND BAKE

Necesitamos instalar los artefactos de baño.
[neh-seh-see-TAH-mos ehn-stah-LAHR lohs ahr-teh-FAHK-tohs deh BAHN-yoh]
We need to put in the bathroom fixtures.

Necesitan poner el inodoro aquí.
[neh-seh-SEE-tahn poh-NEHR ehl ehn-oh-DOHR-oh ah-KEE.]
You guys need to put the toilet here.

Ellos necesitan instalar el *sink* (lavabo).
[EH-yohs neh-seh-SEE-tahn ehn-stah-LAHR ehl SEEN (ehl lah-VAH-boh].
They need to install the sink.

Necesita medir y cortar el tubo de drenaje.
[neh-seh-SEE-tah meh-DEER ee kohr-TAHR ehl TOO-boh deh dreh-NAH-heh]
You need to measure and cut the drainpipe.

Ojo. Necesita roscarlo ahora.
[OH-ho. ney-say-SEE-tah rohs-KAHR-loh ah-OHR-ah]
Don't forget. You need to thread it now.

Mire. Necesita unir el drenaje y la trampa.
[MEER-eh. neh-seh-SEE-tah oo-NEER ehl drehn-AH-hey ee lah TRAHM-pah]
Watch. You need to join the drain and trap.

Necesitan conexiones de lavaplatos y lavadora.
[ney-say-SEE-tahn kohn-eks-ee-OHN-ehs deh lah-vah-PLAH-tohs ee lah-vah-DOHR-ah]
You'll need dishwasher and washing machine connections.

SECTION II

Lesson 10: Look Who's Talking

Wasn't that Section I fun stuff? Until now you've been learning how to *communicate* all kinds of useful things right from the git-go, and without any homework, tests, or D-minuses in the grade book. However, since we *are* using the honor system here, this might be a good time for a reality check. Think hard about where you are at this point, and mark the appropriate box:

My Personal Progress

☐ *a.* I'm with the program (babbling like a fool in Spanish—*necesito* this and *necesitan* that—all over the job site). I'm ready to move on.

☐ *b.* I'm working hard at memorizing the stuff, but still too scared to open my mouth and try any of it at work.

☐ *c.* I've just been reading along (enjoying the obviously charming literary style of this book) but that's about all.

☐ *d.* None of the above. Someone gave me this book as a gift, and I've been using it as a doorstop.

If you marked *b*, *c*, or *d* (or even if you marked *a*, but were lying to yourself), you need to spend more time in Section I. But don't worry. There are no time limits here, no final exams or semester breaks coming up. You don't even have to forge a note saying the dog ate your homework. It's your book, you bought it, and you can take all the time you want in getting through it. My only advice here is not to move forward until you're ready. This really is like building a house—if you insist on starting the framing before the foundation is poured, you're gonna have problems. For those of you who honestly have Section I under control, we are going to be cranking things up a few notches in this section.

Now that you are getting pretty good at using *necesitar* with the base form of other verbs to say things which are actually understood, you have probably noticed that something is still missing. Like, for starters, everyone nods, smiles, and tries to let you know how well you are speaking Spanish, but that's about as far as it goes. When *they* decide to start talking, you can't understand anything they are saying. Downright *clueless* would be a fair description of how you feel, right? They could be speaking Russian or Tibetan for all you know. Secondly, you have discovered that not everything you want to say can possibly start with *I need to, you need to,* etc. For even simple things like "Hi, how are you?", asking "how you need to be?" really doesn't cut it.

Let's not get depressed about this (at least, not yet!). Actually, these two problems are very closely connected. It's just that your Spanish-speaking co-workers already know how to use a whole lot of other verbs in the same way we have been using *necesitar*. This section is about helping you get to where they are with verbs, because—get ready for it, heeeere it comes—*verb usage is the real key to language, any language.* Man, that is so profound it bears repeating: *Get the verbs and the rest of it is a piece o' cake.* Verbs are the glue that holds language together— you can't get any action without them. Even the basics like *breathing, scratching,* and *belching* are verb forms, know what I mean?

So, where do we start? Well, unless you have been sleeping in class, you should know that we have already made a pretty good start in Section I. Let's take a minute to recap what you already know about Spanish verbs (which is quite a lot, actually!):

- You know that, like English verbs, there is a base form (the *infinitive*, the "idling engine").

- You know that there are six possibilities for **who** to match a verb's **action**, three singular and three plural:

Singular	Plural
yo (I)	**nosotros** (we)
usted (you)	**ustedes** (you guys)
él/ella (he/she)	**ellos/ellas** (they)

- You know that there are really only *four* endings for the six possibilities, so we can simplify even further:

Singular	Plural
yo	**nosotros**
usted,él,ella	**ustedes,ellos,ellas**

- With *necesitar*, you are actually using these possibilities with a real Spanish verb.

- You have also learned at least the base (infinitive) form of a number of other useful verbs.

All things considered, not a bad start! You are already way ahead of anyone who ignored our offer and signed up for Spanish 1A in their local diploma mill. They are just now beginning to bumble and stumble their way through such cutting-edge stuff as "Good morning", "how are you", and "my name is Pedro." (By the way, we *will* get to those eventually, but our feeling is that none of that stuff is

129

going to get a stud nailed to a plate so that everyone gets paid this week.)

FOR ALL YOU REALLY ANAL FOLKS

Spanish, like English, has both very specific rules on how verbs work, and a fair number of verbs which are rule-breakers, choosing to *do their own thing*, so to speak. O.K., so here's the thing. We are going to blow all that off, because trying to learn all the rules, what ifs, and no-nos just ain't a good way of learning any verbs. Did any of you learn English by going to grammar classes when you were still in diapers? I'm guessing that the answer here is "no". However, now that I have mentioned rules and exceptions, some of you will just have to know what all these are, or you're going to get irritable, worry a lot, and lose sleep. To find out if you are one of those, try mentally answering *yes* or *no* to the following questions:

- Do you always read the instructions first?

- Do you consciously avoid stepping on cracks in the sidewalk?

- Do you subtract the tax from your restaurant bill before figuring out the tip?

- Does it seem important to you to know that tornadoes spin counterclockwise in the Northern Hemisphere, but clockwise in the Southern Hemisphere?

- Have you ever seriously worried about why they put Braille on drive-through bank machines?

If you answered yes to any of these scientifically selected questions, then admit it—you probably are pretty anal about things, but hey, that's O.K. Appendix C in the back of the book will give you a lengthy rundown on verb mechanics that you can memorize to protect your mental health. Everyone else is free to skip it if they want, 'cuz we aren't gonna use any of it anyway, and here's why:

THE WAY <u>NOT</u> TO LEARN VERBS

Absolutely the *worst* way of learning verbs is the way most language programs try to teach them, which goes something like this:

- Memorize all the verb mechanics we give you in Appendix C for both regular and irregular verbs of all types.

- Memorize the base form, the infinitive, of each verb you need to learn.

- As you are speaking, try to think ahead to what verb you are going to need to complete your sentence, (analyzing at the same time whether you are going to need the *I, you, he, we,* or *they* form), then apply the mechanics—the "rules"—to come up with the right form in Spanish.

- While you're at it, don't forget to worry the whole time whether the verb you need is, in fact, regular and actually follows the rules, or whether it happens to be irregular and you are going to screw the whole thing up anyway.

- And finally, you are of course expected to do all this while speaking at a normal pace, without any long pauses in each sentence which make you look and feel like a complete dummy!

I dare you—no, I *double dog dare you*--to try following this process every time you open your mouth to say something, for *every* stinking verb in *every* sentence. Unless you are some kind of linguistic Houdini, you will experience the same brain freeze as everyone else who ever tried to learn Spanish and gave up. If you are like me, by the time you sort it all out, you will have most likely forgotten what you were trying to say in the first place. So, screw this method, it doesn't work. Let's go back to the diaper approach, or what the language specialists call the "natural approach"—it obviously worked for us once, so why wouldn't it work again?

The reason why little kids can learn language, even more than one language, quicker than we "smart" adults is because *they don't try to memorize all the stupid rules* before speaking. Kids learn "on the fly"—meaning they hear and imitate verbs as they are actually being used, without even knowing that any rules exist. I say go with what works, and 1-year-old to 4-year-old kids, worldwide, are the only real experts in learning to speak quickly and naturally. They don't always get it exactly right when they start, but we are able to understand them, and they get better and better with practice.

TWO-MINUTE DRILL — BACKGROUND

O.K., one more time. We know one regular verb, *necesitar*, right? And we memorized **o, a, amos, an** (*necesito, necesita, necesitamos, necesitan*) in order to put it to work. All regular verbs ending in –ar work this way, so a really useful verb like *clavar* (to nail) is going to be clavo, clava, clavamos, clavan. With me so far? Good. Now, maybe you noticed in Section I that not all the verb infinitives ended in –ar, or maybe you just thought I couldn't spell or type. While most Spanish verbs end in –ar, some end in –er or –ir. Don't let this throw you, 'cause it ain't that different.

Where -**ar** verbs use **o, a, amos, an**, verbs ending in -**er** use **o, e, emos, en**. Makes sense, right? We use **a** endings for –**ar** verbs, and **e** for –**er** verbs. As an example of a useful verb ending in –**er**, let's use *barrer* (to sweep)— barro, barre, barremos, barren. All regular –**er** verbs work the same way.

To make things even easier, as we mention in Appendix C, verbs ending in –ir are really nothing more than wannabe –er verbs with one small difference. The endings for –ir verbs are **o, e, imos, en.** Just like the verbs ending in –er, except for the "we" form, where they go to –imos instead of **-emos.** Let's face it, your pronunciation is never going to be perfect anyway, so if you forget and use **-emos** for –ir verbs, it's no big thing. You will be understood. An example of a useful verb ending in –ir is **unir** (*to join* or *connect*)—**uno, une, unimos, unen.**

Irregular verbs are another story—every language has them, and they are difficult to learn by traditional methods (*see "How Not to Learn Verbs", above*), because they don't follow the rules. Most irregular Spanish verbs simply have some spelling changes in some of the forms, to reflect how they are actually pronounced today, in the 21st century—some of them might have even been regular a few hundred years ago, but changed as the way people talk changed.

For God's sake, don't stress over any of this. The only reason for even telling you about it is to make what follows a little easier. If you use our method, all this will come together for you without a lot of extra effort on your part.

TACKLING VERBS "NATURALLY"

The very best way to master verbs is to learn them the way they actually are, and are used, without trying to understand whether they are regular, irregular, left- or right-handed, or always vote Republican. Learn each verb right the first time, and nothing else really matters—not even the rules. By learning, I mean *memorize* each one, one at a time, as you need them. It will go a little slow at first, but once you have memorized a few, the others will come much faster with experience. Some of you are going to get nervous here, thinking you will never be able to learn all these strange-sounding words, which is what has always scared you away from trying to learn another language.

The truth is that you can *and do* learn all kinds of strange-sounding words anyway—in English, and without getting hung up on *why* they are the way they are. You have been doing this throughout your career in construction. Remember your first week on your very first job, when someone maybe asked you to do something with a *joist?* Did you say to yourself, "My, what an interesting word. I need to research where it came from in order to really understand it"? I mean, did you really care if it came from some ancient Celtic tribal word for the pelvic bone of a yak used to support the roof of their teepee? Get real--of course not. I'm guessing you said, "What's a joist?" (Actually, what I said was, "Who is this Joyce, and can we get arrested for doing that?" Shows you where my mind was!) And when you found out what a joist was, you just went with it. Same thing with words like *caulking, coping, dormer, gypsum, lapping, mastic, nosings, plenum, rebar, soffit, tendons,* and *truss.* Not your everyday English words, but you learned them when you needed them, and the more you used them, the easier they were to remember.

We are first going to introduce you to a nifty bit of shorthand to help you *visualize* verbs in Spanish. Throughout the remainder of the book, we will use the following "graphic" form to introduce verbs. For the four forms we need to learn, the left side of our visual will always contain the two singular forms and the right side will contain the two plurals:

yo	nosotros
usted*, él, ella	ustedes, ellos, ellas

Remember we are not using the informal **tú form just to simplify things. Refer to Section I pages 17-18 for a full explanation.*

Using the same three sample regular verbs we just introduced you to, it looks something like this:

CLAVAR
to nail

clavo	clavamos
clava	clavan

BARRER
to sweep

barro	barremos
barre	barren

UNIR
to join or connect

uno	unimos
une	unen

Using this format, you can make your own nifty flash cards to help you memorize *any* Spanish verb you need to know. Get a pack of blank 3 x 5 cards, and use one card for each verb you want. On one side put the English verb, like *to nail*, on the reverse, put the Spanish verb exactly like the examples above. Work back and forth between the two sides of the card until you have the Spanish verb memorized. Let's see, I need to know the Spanish verb for *to nail*, so I am going to use the graphic to memorize:

to nail = CLAVAR: clavo, clava, clavamos, clavan.

The base verb, along with the four forms in the graphic, is all you need to learn in order to use any verb, regular or irregular, in the present tense. Here are a few examples of useful verbs which happen to be irregular, to show you how the graphic will help you learn them as well:

PONER
to put or place

pong<u>o</u>	ponemos
pone	ponen

MEDIR
to measure

m<u>i</u>do	medimos
m<u>i</u>de	m<u>i</u>den

CONTAR
to count

c<u>ue</u>nto	contamos
c<u>ue</u>nta	c<u>ue</u>ntan

Appendix B gives you a long list of important verbs in this format, including those that are irregular. (Stick to the left column of Appendix B, the present tense, for now. We'll get to the past and future a little later.) *By memorizing each verb as it actually is,* you don't need to worry about whether it is regular or not—it will always be the way you learned it, and that's all you need to know. Rules? What rules? I just learn verbs!

With the ability to use more verbs in the way we are using necesitar, we open up a whole new world of ways to say things with the vocabulary we already know:

Por favor, claven ustedes el subpiso [*subflor*].
Would you guys nail down the subfloor, please.

Pablo, barre el piso, por favor.
Pablo, sweep the floor, please.

Juan y Carlos barren el piso.
Juan and Carlos sweep (or are sweeping) the floor.

Bueno. Ahora unimos los tubos.
Good. Now we connect the pipes.

Don't worry if all this isn't totally clicking with you right now. Keep plugging through the remainder of Section II, and by that point you should be comfortably making and using flash cards for the verbs you need the most to communicate in a way that makes the most sense to you. My advice is to take it slow—trying to memorize and use too many verbs at once is a good way to get frustrated and discouraged. Like every other skill we want to acquire, we have to learn to crawl before we can learn to walk (and even run!).

Lesson 11: "To Be, or Not to Be . . ."

O.K., so much for Shakespeare—never much cared for the guy anyway. Dressed kinda funny, know what I mean? The dude ran around wearing tights and those pointy shoes—what was that all about? Ballet *maybe*, but hangin' with the construction gang—*I don't think so*. Anyway, the quote works as a title, because in English the verb *to be* is really not *to be*. Here's what I'm getting at. If you look at your average, everyday English verb, like *to yodel* for example, you see an immediate pattern:

<u>Singular</u>	<u>Plural</u>
I **yodel**	we **yodel**
you **yodel**	you guys **yodel**
he/she/it **yodel<u>s</u>**	they **yodel**

Simple, right? Just use the base verb without the *to*, and add an *–s* when you get to he, she, or it. That's the way our verbs are supposed to work. However, for *to be*, we have

I **am** — (not I **be**)

you **are** — (instead of you **be**)

he/she/it **is** — (not **bes**)

What genius came up with this winner? How can this be *to be*, when none of the forms even contain the letter b. Apparently, as mankind's very first verb, it just sorta happened. *To be* was probably around for a few thousand years before anyone cared about yodeling, or about organizing their verbs for that matter. *Soooo,* we learn to live with it.

To tackle the verb *to be* in Spanish, we first need to get you in the right frame of mind. We all learn better when we have a clear picture of where we're going and are really jazzed about getting there, right? So, here's the key—try thinking of learning the verb *to be* as kinda like playing poker with the Mafia. All you have to do is memorize these three simple rules:

You can't win.

You can't break even.

You can't fold.

There, don't you feel better now that you know the plan? HEY! PUT THE NAIL GUNS DOWN! I'm just having a little fun with you here—we really are going to help you through this.

THE SPANISH "TO BE"

First, the really big news. There are actually *two* verbs for "to be" in Spanish. *"Oh, my gawd!"* I hear you say, *"What could be worse?"* Well, for starters, they are both irregular, like the English. This means you need to memorize *both the verbs and a few simple rules* about when to use which (or is it which to use when? I can never remember). Anyway, here they both be:

ESTAR
to be

estoy	estamos
está	están

SER
to be

soy	somos
es	son

ESTAR

As you can see, *estar* pretty much follows the *-ar* verb rules which you learned for *necesitar*, except for I/yo, where a "*y*" is tacked onto the end, making it *estoy* instead of *esto*. Not too tough so far, but now for the really important part—when to use it.

Estar is the *immediate*, "*touchy-feely*" version of "to be". It describes something or someone's state, condition, taste, or feelings *at a given moment*. Examples include

Estoy enfermo.	I **am** sick ("I don't feel good").
El **está** felíz.	He **is** happy.
Está bien.	That **is** O.K., or that **is** good.
Estamos ocupados.	We **are** busy ("occupied").
¿Cómo **está** el café? **Está** frío.	How **is** the coffee? It **is** cold.
¿Cómo **está** usted? **Estoy** bien.	How **are** you? I **am** fine.

You will note that none of these describe any relatively unchanging **characteristics** of anything—like being tall, short, ugly, red, dumb, etc. What we have described are current **conditions**, which could easily change. In the above examples, *estoy enfermo,* but I could take an aspirin and start feeling better; *el está feliz,* but kick him in the unmentionables, and he won't be real happy anymore; heat the coffee and it won't stay cold. Estar does not describe what something basically *is* —only how it is acting, feeling, doing, or appearing at the time.

Estar is also always used to express physical or geographical locations:

141

¿Dónde **está** mi martillo? **Está** allí.	Where **is** my hammer? It **is** over there.
Miami **está** en Florida.	Miami **is** in Florida.
El baño **está** en el segundo piso.	The bathroom **is** upstairs.

This is pretty much what you need for the basics of *estar*. Remember **Condition** (what is going on with it), and **Location** (where is it physically situated). Got it so far? Good, because we are now going to move on to *ser*, the "other" *to be* verb.

SER

This one is a little more irregular than estar, but still not a real killer. In fact, when you are talking to or about a single person or thing (which is most of the time), the **es** form is almost the same as the English **is**. So close that, if you blow it and use the English *is*, no one is going to make a big thing of it.

As far as uses of **ser**, it would be easy to say "use it for everything except for what we already told you requires **estar**". However, we are going to go a whole lot further, and give you the major times when **ser** is the one to use:

• **Ser** is used for ownership or possession.

Es mi coche.	It **is** my car.
¿De quién **es** el martillo.	Whose hammer **is** this?

Ser is used when describing what something is made of.

¿De qué **es** la puerta?	What **is** the door made of?

Es de roble.	It **is** oak.
Mi teléfono **es** de plástico.	My phone **is** plastic.

- **Ser** is always used to express time—hour, day and date.

¿Qué hora **es**?	What time **is** it
Son las tres.	It **is** three o'clock.
Es la una.	It **is** one o'clock.
¿Qué día **es** hoy?	What day **is** today?
Es sábado.	It **is** Saturday.
¿Qué fecha **es** mañana?	What **is** the date tomorrow?
Es el dos de febrero.	It **is** February 2nd.

You should note two things about telling time in Spanish. The hours are aways feminine, and only one o'clock is singular (which makes sense--one *is* singular, right?). Everything else is more than one, and therefore has to be plural, so you get **la una**, but **las dos**, **las tres**, etc.

- **Ser** is used to express occupation.

¿Qué **es** usted?	What **is** your trade or profession?
Soy carpintero.	I **am** a carpenter.
Mi esposa **es** maestra.	My wife **is** a teacher.
Ellos **son** ruferos.	Those guys **are** roofers.

143

You may note that the question ¿Qué es usted? literally translates as *What are you?* This question *always* means what do you *do for a living,* and that is the only answer you should give. Don't get tempted to be a smart aleck—answers like **loco** (*crazy*) or **divorciado y feliz** (*divorced and happy*) will not win you any points. In fact, I probably shouldn't have mentioned it, because some of you will now be thinking up your own off-the-wall answers. Oh, well.

- **Ser** is used to express nationality and where someone is from.

El **es** mexicano.	He **is** Mexican.
¿**Es** usted mexicano?	**Are** you Mexican?
No. **Soy** puertorriqueño.	No. I **am** Puerto Rican.
¿De dónde **son** ellos?	Where **are** they from?
Son de Mexico.	They **are** from Mexico.
Soy de Los Angeles.	I **am** from Los Angeles.

- **Ser** is the verb of choice for politics and religion and marital status. (Of course, if you don't think your marriage is going to last long, you are free to use *estar* instead of *ser*, indicating that marriage, for you, is a *temporary condition* and not an *unchanging characteristic.*)

¿**Es** usted católico?	**Are** you Catholic?
No. **Soy** bautista.	No. I **am** Baptist.
Somos republicanos.	We **are** Republicans.

Ellos **son** demócratas.	They **are** Democrats.
Soy casado.	I **am** married.
Ella **es** mi esposa.	She **is** my wife ("spouse").
Juan **es** divorciado.	Juan **is** divorced.

Unlike the examples for estar, you will note that none of these deal with emotions, feelings, or things which come and go *easily*. They describe relatively unchanging **characteristics**—the core materials, so to speak. Unless your feelings about marriage are that it is a temporary thing, then you can use **Estoy casado** instead of **Soy casado**. But use it at your discretion. We are not responsible for the consequences.

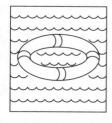

If this whole concept of *characteristic* versus *condition* just doesn't float your boat, you might try this simple memory key. Think of *estar* as answering the question **How**, while *ser* answers the question **What**. "My car is parked across the street" will use *estar*, because we are talking about **how** it is *currently* situated (location). "My car is red" will use *ser*, because that's **what** it is—red. "I am pissed off" will use *estar*, because that's **how** I am *feeling* right now. "I am a contractor" will use *ser*, because that's **what** I am.

SIMPLIFY THE USE OF ESTAR (AND SER)

There is one fact about the use of verbs in Spanish which can help you to simplify the use of the verb **estar** (and **ser**). There are two different verb forms for the present tense: one is the *present simple* and the other is the *present progressive*. For example: we can say "I *do* something" and "I *am doing* something" such as follows:

145

Present	Present Progressive (always uses the verb **estar**)
I sweep the floor. **Barro el piso.**	I am sweeping the floor. **Estoy barriendo el piso.**
You drive a car. **Usted maneja el carro.**	You are driving a car. **Usted está manejando el carro.**
They eat dinner early. **Ellos cenan temprano.**	They are eating right now. **Ellos están cenando ahora mismo.**

Although both forms are different, many times the first form, which is the present tense you are learning, *is commonly used for both forms*. You can frequently avoid the *to be* (**estar**) verb by sticking to the verb which describes the action you want, knowing that it already includes the *am, is* or *are* that we would have to tack on in English. For example, in Spanish:

(**Yo**) *barro* is taken to mean both "I sweep" AND "I am sweeping".

(**Nosotros**) *clavamos* is taken to mean both "We nail" AND "We are nailing".

(**Ellos**) *levantan* is taken to mean both "They lift" AND "They are lifting".

Understanding this will help you understand some of the "mistakes" made by your native Spanish-speaking co-workers who are struggling to learn English. When you ask something such as, "Where are you *going*?" you often get an answer like "I *go* to the doctor." That's because it makes perfect sense in Spanish, where that same conversation would be:

"¿A donde va?" (which would be understood as "Where **are** you **going**?" not "Where you **go**?")

"Voy al doctor." ("I **am going** to the doctor", not "I **go** to the doctor".)

In learning to speak Spanish, all we have to do is practice using the verb that is carrying the action, without trying to complicate things by throwing in forms of **(estar)** *to be*. Bottom line is, we only use **estar** or **ser** when either *is actually the verb carrying the action*, which is the case when we want to say something like *"How are you?"* **(¿Cómo está?)**, or *"What time is it?"* **(¿Que hora es?)**.

Always focusing on the *action-carrying verb* not only helps me keep my own sentences simple, but helps me big time in understanding what other people are saying to me in Spanish. With practice, it becomes so natural that I find myself wondering why we don't do the same thing in English. Trust me; it's a lot harder going from Spanish to English on this, than it is moving from English to Spanish.

When memorizing new Spanish verbs, we recommend to repeat both of these uses to constantly remind yourself not to think in English and then try to translate things word for word into Spanish. For example, when working on a handy verb such as **Usar**— *to use*, do the four forms like this:

uso (I use, I am using)	*usamos* (we use, we are using)
usa (you use, you are using) (he/she uses, he/she is using)	*usan* (you guys use, you guys are using) (they use, they are using)

You may find another method that works just as well for you, but we recommend reminding yourself of the two meanings as you memorize each form of a verb. This will help you stick to the action verb as you speak—without trying to wedge in *estar* or *ser* where it is not needed for basic communication.

AND, FINALLY . . .

Don't get so hung up on getting it right, that you are afraid to open your mouth and try. Most native Spanish speakers on the job site have made, or are making some efforts to learn a little English, so they know it ain't easy. They will appreciate your efforts, and will generally help you along. Since *ser* and *estar* both mean *to be*, you will get your point across, even if you sometimes use the wrong one, or didn't really need to use either one. Just keep plugging, and pretty soon it will come naturally—*even as weird as it be.*

Lesson 12: **The Dirty Dozen**

(give or take a few)

Sorry, guys, forget the movie. We're still talking verbs here, and anyway, the publisher shot down my idea of putting a bag of popcorn in the back of the book. *Yeah, I know*—you deserve a break after wrestling with all that when to use **estar** and when to use **ser** stuff, but I promise you that what I am going to give you here will be really useful (dull as dirt, maybe, but really *useful!*). Spanish, like English or any other language, has something like a gazillion verbs, but here's the thing. Only a small number are really important for basic everyday communication. Think about it. In English, how many times a day do you use verbs like *to be, do, go, say, have, want, work, know,* etc.? In comparison, how often are you going to use *to oscillate, desiccate,* or *emasculate*? I rest my case. A small number of verbs drive most of what we need to say, and we are going to give you some of the biggies here, along with examples of how they get used.

You are going to note that a lot of these verbs have some little quirks (O.K., let's not sugarcoat it—they're irregular). It's like we explained to you about the verb *to be.* Most of the verbs we are talking about here were useful even to cavemen, who were too busy fighting off saber-tooth tigers to give a rat's patootie about grammar. It's the same in every language—these kinds of verbs got there first, and the rules came later. But, hey, we are going to memorize them *exactly the way they are*, so regular or irregular doesn't really matter.

Número uno

HACER
to do, to make

hago	hacemos
hace	hacen

¿Qué hacen ustedes?
What are you guys doing?
Por favor, hágalo ahora.
Please do it now.
No haga eso, por favor.
Please don't do that.
Hoy hacemos las formas.
Today we are making the (foundation) forms.
Yo hago cualquier trabajo.
I do any kind of work.

Número dos

PODER
to be able to, "can"

puedo	podemos
puede	pueden

¿Puede hacerlo?
Can you do it?
¿Puede trabajar mañana?
Can you work tomorrow?
No puedo.
I can't [do it].
¿Pueden levantarlo un poco?
Can you guys lift it up a little?
Podemos hacerlo mañana.
We can do that tomorrow.

Número tres

QUERER
to want, to want to

quiero	queremos
quiere	quieren

Quiero hacerlo, pero no puedo.
I want to do it, but I can't.
¿Quiere trabajar mañana?
Do you want to work tomorrow?
¿Qué quieren ellos?
What do they want?
¿Cómo queremos hacer esto?
How do we want to do this?
Mire. Quiero un poco de ayuda aquí.
Hey. I want a little help here.

Número cuatro

1. TENER
to have

tengo	tenemos
tiene	tienen

2. TENER QUE
to "have to"

tengo que	tenemos que
tiene que	tienen que

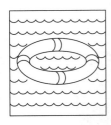

No reason to panic here. Spanish, like English, uses *to have* in terms of *possession*, as well as *to have to*, meaning *must*. For example, I could say, **"Porque *tengo* una novia, *tengo que* comportarme bien."** ("Because I *have* a girlfriend, I *have to* behave myself.") Got it? Anytime you use **tener** by itself, it means to have (to possess), and when you want to say "have to", you use **tener que**.

> **Tengo un troque nueva.**
> *I have a new pickup.*
> **Tenemos que trabajar mañana.**
> *We have to work tomorrow.*
> **¿Tiene un martillo?**
> *Do you have a hammer?*
> **Ellos tienen que hacerlo ahorita.**
> *They have to do it right now.*
> **¿Tienen suficuentes clavos?**
> *Do you guys have enough nails?*

Número cinco

PONER
to put, to place

pon**go**	ponemos
pone	ponen

Por favor, ponga eso en mi troque.
Put that in my truck, please.
Ahora ponemos el piso.
We are putting the floor in now.
Ojo. Ellos ponen las vigas.
Heads up. They are putting in the beams.
¿Dónde ponen la puerta?
Where are you guys putting the door?

Número seis

DAR
to give

d<u>oy</u>	damos
da	dan

Me da unos clavos, por favor.
Give me some nails, please.

or, **Me da un *bonche* de clavos, por favor.**
Give me a "handful" of nails.
Doy una hora para *lonchar.*
I give an hour lunch break.
Por favor, me dan los números de telefóno.
I need all of your phone numbers.

Número siete

1. VENIR
to come

ven<u>go</u>	venimos
v<u>i</u>ene	v<u>i</u>enen

2. IR
to go

v<u>oy</u>	vamos
va	van

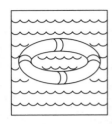

Combining these two goes back to my belief that it is easier to memorize opposites (i.e., come/go, up/down, here/there, etc.) together rather than separately. In this set, *ya' gotta really watch ir*, 'cuz it's probably the most irregular verb in the Spanish language. (Pretty weird in English, too, by the way. I mean, how do we get from *I go* to *I went*?) The only way to master the verb *ir* is to forget logic and memorize, memorize, *memorize*.

Vengo a las seis todos los días.
I come ("get here") at six every day.
Voy a la ferretería ahora.
I am going to the hardware store now.
Carlos viene los sábados.
Carlos comes on Saturdays.
¿Van todos mañana?
Are you guys all going tomorrow?
Venimos aquí a trabajar, no a platicar.
We come here to work, not B.S.
Vamos al otro sitio ésta tarde.
We're going to the other job site this after-noon.

Número ocho

DECIR
to say, to tell

di**go**	de**cimos**
di**ce**	d**i**cen

¿Qúe dice?
What's that you're saying?
Digo que necesitamos empezar.
I say we need to get started.
Ellos dicen que no pueden hacerlo.
They say they can't do it.

Juan dice que no puede.
Juan says that he can't do it.
Decimos eso, pero nunca lo hacemos.
We say that, but we never do it.
¿Dicen que están listos?
Are you guys telling me you're ready?

Número nueve

SABER
to know

sé	sabemos
sabe	saben

Lo sé, pero ¿qúe podemos hacer?
I know that, but what can we do?
¿Sabe cómo hacerlo?
Do you know how to do it?
Ellos saben como hacer eso.
They know how to do that.
No sabemos si Pedro viene o no.
We don't know if Pedro is coming or not.
Yo lo sé, y usted lo sabe, pero ¿lo saben ellos?
I know it, and you know it, but do they?

Número diez

LLEVAR
to bring, to carry

llevo	llevamos
lleva	llevan

Lléveme más montantes, por favor.
Bring me some more studs, please.
Llevan esos al segundo piso.
Carry those up to the second floor.

155

Ellos llevan la revolvedora.
They're bringing the cement mixer .
¡Ojo! Llevamos madera aquí.
Heads up! We're carrying lumber here.
Llévalo allí, por favor.
Bring it there, please.

Número once

TRABAJAR
to work

trabajo	trabajamos
trabaja	trabajan

Hoy trabajamos hasta las siete.
We're working until seven today.
Juan, trabaja con Pedro ésta mañana.
Juan, work with Pedro this morning.
Ellos no trabajan sin café.
Those guys don't work without coffee.
¿Trabaja este sábado, o no?
Are you working this Saturday, or not?
Es más facil si trabajan juntos.
It's a lot easier if you guys work together.

Número doce

1. LLAMAR
to call, to "knock"

llamo	llamamos
llama	llaman

2. LLAMARSE
to be called (named)

me llamo	**nos** llamamos
se llama	**se** llaman

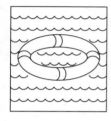

Oh, yeah! We definitely be needin' a life ring on this one! Spanish has a second version of many verbs, which all look like the first version, but with this "se" tacked on the end. These are called *reflexive* verbs, and are used to indicate that the verb's action is doin' its thing on the subject of the sentence. Got that?

No, I didn't think so. It is used when I want to indicate I'm doing something *to myself*, or that I am describing something that someone else is doing *to himself*. As an example, let's look at a verb you already know, such as *levantar*, to lift or raise. If I am sitting down, and want to say that I am getting up, it would be correct to use *llevantarse*, and say, "me levanto"—literally, "I am lifting *myself* up". (No one is doing this for me, right? It is up to me to haul my own butt out of the chair.)

Although the reflexive form of certain verbs is really correct in certain circumstances, like the one I just described, it's not like you can't communicate without them. Most of the time you will be understood when you use the normal verb.

However, *llamar* and *llamarse* are a bit of an important special case, because both are used a lot, and *mean different things*. Llamar is used when talking about calling someone, especially on the phone, and *llamar a la puerta* means to knock on the door, which sorta makes sense, because you knock to "call" someone to the door. We carry this meaning in English too, when we "answer the door"—we're responding to someone's "call". Examples include:

Llámeme a casa a las siete.
Call me at home at seven o'clock.

Si no le llamo, es que no hay trabajo.
If I don't call, it means there's no work.

Por favor, llame usted a Juan.
Would you please call Juan?

Por favor, *llámelo para atrás.* *
Call him back, please.

*This is pure *Spanglish* copying the English of calling someone "back". Proper Spanish is "to return someone's call", **devolver la llamada**, but nearly everybody either uses or at least understands the *Spanglish*, **llamar por atrás**, so why not go with it?

Llamarse is an important verb in its own right. In Spanish when asking for someone's name we usually say the equivalent of "What (or how) do you call *yourself?*"and the common answer is "I call *myself*...", and that calls for **llamarse**, a reflexive form of the verb which turns the action back on itself. You will get used to this pretty quickly. It goes something like this:

¿Cómo se llama (usted)?
What's your name?

Me llamo Pedro Cervantes.
My name is (or "I'm") Pedro Cervantes.

Se llama José Gonzales.
His name is José Gonzales.

That, in a nutshell, is all you really need to know about llamarse in reference to people's names—first person (I) and third person (you, he, she) in the singular.

The verb **llamarse** is also used for finding the names of things and animals. Here is an important and useful trick to enhance your vocabulary:

As you know (and if not, we are telling you) we go around the universe (micro and macro) naming things. If we don't know their name, it is as if they don't even exist. So the best way is to ask for it. If you get in the habit of going around the workplace repeating **Cómo se llama esto?** (*What is this called?*) and pointing at things to get their names in Spanish, your vocabulary would improve tenfold before you knew it.

Ever Onward

Now that you have mastered a few of these, you have actually accomplished two major things. You have learned some really useful verbs and expressions; equally important, you have learned *how to learn* verbs, using the simple graphic for the four essential forms of each. With the list of verbs we have provided in Appendix B, you can easily knock off any other verb you might need. To show you how this works, we are now going to take a quick run back through building our house, giving you examples of some other verbs whose *infinitive* forms you learned in Section I. (Or did you? I can only throw them out there for you— what you do with them is up to you.) This will give you some options of how to say things, with or without using *necesitar*. Either way will be understood, so go with whatever fits your style of talking. And even if you continue using *necesitar* most of the time, you will know how to use other verbs when "I need", "you need", and "we need" just doesn't fit with what you are trying to say.

Lesson 13: Back to Our House

We have been shoveling a lot of verbs at you, with a few sample sentences for each, but since you must have liked that organized march through the stages of construction that we had in Section I, let's do it again. We are going to revisit our house, picking out some of the **necesitar** sentences and showing you a couple of different ways to say those very same things using other verbs instead. First, flip back a couple of pages to the Dirty Dozen verbs, and look at the verb **tener**. Remember that **tener** by itself means *to have* ("to possess"), but adding **que** to make it **tener que** changes the meaning to *to have to* ("to must", "to be required to"). Saying "you have to" do something is an alternative to saying "you need to" do it. Use **tener que** to add emphasis on the action to say what *must* be done.

The second way is to eliminate **necesitar** (or **tener que**) entirely. You may remember when we introduced *necesitar* the very first time, we talked about sentences with two verbs, like "I **need** to **go** to work", and that only the first verb is changed to identify *who*, while the second verb stays in the infinitive, the "idling mode." Well, once you start using your flash cards to learn the "who" endings on other verbs, you can always go with the actual action verb, without using either **necesitar** or **tener que** as helpers. Instead of saying something like "Today you need to dig the footings", you can simply say, "Today you are digging the footings" (Hoy excava las zapatas), or "Tomorrow we dig the footings" (Mañana excavamos las zapatas).

Following these sentence comparisons, you will have a sample conversation to review, in order to get the feel for how all this comes together in day-to-day communication. Soooo, get out your shovels and trowels, and let's get rolling with the foundation . . . (in case you didn't get the hint, *turn the page, Einstein!*).

FUNDACIONES
(Foundations)

Necesitamos excavar las zapatas.
We need to dig the footings.
Ahora, tenemos que excavar las zapatas.

>**Ahora, excavamos las zapatas.**
>*We are digging the footings now.*

Necesita/necesitan excavarlos.
You/you guys need to dig them.
Tiene que excavarlos.

>**Usted los excava por favor.**
>*Dig them, please.*

Necesita darme el pico.
Hey. I need the pick.
Mire. Tiene que darme el pico.

>**Me da el pico por favor.**
>*Hey. Please give me the pick.*

Necesita usar la pala, no el pico.
You need to use the shovel, not the pick.
Tiene que usar la pala, no el pico.

>**Usa la pala, no el pico.**
>*Use the shovel, not the pick.*

Necesitan instalar las formas.
You/you guys need to put in the forms.
Tienen que instalar las formas.

>**Ustedes instalan las formas, por favor.**
>*Put in the forms. (You/you guys)*

Necesita usar el marro en las estacas.
You need to use the sledge on the stakes.
Tiene que usar el marro en las estacas.

> **Usa el marro en las estacas.**
> *Use the sledge on the stakes.*

Necesita torcerlo.
You need to twist it.
Tiene que torcerlo.

> **Usted lo tuerce así.**
> *Twist it like this.*

Ojo. Él necesita pompear el cemento.
Heads up. He needs to pump the cement.
Ojo. Él tiene que pompear el cemento.

> **Ojo. Él pompea el cemento.**
> *Heads up. He's pumping the cement.*

Necesita allanarlo.
You need to trowel it.
Tiene que allanarlo.

> **Allánelo, por favor.**
> *Trowel it.*

Sample Dialogue

You: **Pedro, instala las formas, por favor.**
Pedro, put in the foundation forms.
Pedro: **Bueno. ¿Cómo hago eso?**
Yeah, O.K. How do I do that?
You: **¿Por qué no usa el marro?**
Why don't you use the sledge?

163

Pedro:	**Está bien. ¿Y, entonces?**
	O.K. Then what?
You:	**Ayuda a Juan con las barras.**
	Help Juan with the rebar.
Pedro:	**¿Dónde está el alambre?**
	Where's the wire?
You:	**En mi troque. Traelo aquí.**
	In my truck. Bring it here.
Pedro:	**Aquí está. Puedo usar estas pinzas?**
	Here it is. Can I use these pliers?
You:	**Sí. (Claro que sí)**
	Yes. (Of course)

FREIMEANDO
(Framing)

Necesitamos poner las vigas de piso.
We need to put in the floor joists.
Tenemos que poner las vigas del piso.

> **Hoy ponemos las vigas de piso.**
> *We're putting in the floor joists today.*

Necesita/Necesitan medir y cortarlos.
You/you guys need to measure and cut them.
Tiene/tienen que cortarlos y medirlos.

> **Mide y córtalos/los miden y los cortan.**
> *Cut them. (You/you guys)*

Mire. Necesita clavarlos en ángulo.
Watch. You need to toenail them.
Tiene que clavarlos en ángulo.

> **Clávalos en ángulo.**
> *Watch. Toenail them.*

164

Necesitan clavar los montantes en las placas.
Now, you guys need to nail the studs to the (sill) plates.
Ahora tienen que clavar los montantes en las placas.

> **Ahora clavan los montantes en las placas.**
> *Nail the studs to the plates. (You guys)*

Necesita traerme un bonche de clavos.
You need to bring me a bunch of nails.
Tiene que traerme un bonche de clavos.

> **Me trae un bonche de clavos.**
> *Bring me a bunch of nails.*

Necesita instalar el cabezal.
You need to install the header.
Tiene que instalar el cabezal.

> **Instala el cabezal.**
> *Put in the header.*

Necesita cuadrarlo.
You need to square it up.
Tiene que cuadrarlo.

> **Cuádralo.**
> *Square it up.*

Necesitan suspender las vigas.
You guys need to hang the ceiling joists.
Tienen que suspender las vigas.

> **Suspendan las vigas, por favor.**
> *Hang the ceiling joists. (You guys)*

Necesita cortar y clavar los cabrios.
You need to cut and nail in the rafters.
Tiene que cortar y clavar lo cabrios.

> **Corta y clava los cabrios.**
> *Cut and nail in the rafters.*

Sample Dialogue

You: **Carlos, tenemos que instalar las vigas del piso.**
Carlos, we're installing the floor joists.

Carlos: **¿Necesito medir y cortarlos?**
Do I need to measure and cut them?

You: **No, Juan hace eso.**
No, Juan is doing that.

Carlos: **OK. ¿Tenemos bastantes clavos?**
O.K. Do we have enough nails?

You: **Sí. Abre esa caja nueva.**
Yes. Open that new box.

Carlos: **¿Pueden Juan y Pedro llevar las vigas?**
Can Juan and Pedro carry the joists?

You: **Juan puede, pero Pedro no está aquí.**
Juan can, but Pedro isn't here.

Carlos: **Bueno. ¿Cómo los clavamos?**
O.K. How are we nailing them?

You: **Tienen que clavarlos de ángulo.**
You guys need to toenail them.

ACABADO
(Finish Work)

Necesitan instalar las jambas.
You guys need to install the door jambs.
Tienen que instalar las jambas.

> **Ustedes instalan las jambas.**
> *Install the door jambs (you guys).*

Necesita poner una cuña aquí.
You need to shim it right here.
Tiene que poner una cuña aquí.

> **Pones una cuña aquí.**
> *Look. Shim it (put in a shim) right here.*

Ahora necesita montar las bisagras.
Now you need to mount the hinges.
Ahora tiene que montar las bisagras.

> **Bueno. Ahora, monta las bisagras.**
> *Good. Now mount the hinges.*

Pedro, necesita colgar las puertas.
Pedro, you need to hang the doors.
Pedro, tiene que poner las puertas por favor

> **Pedro, cuelga las puertas, por favor.**
> *Pedro, hang the doors, please.*

Necesitan instalar la baranda.
You guys need to install the banister.
Pedro y Juan, tienen que instalar la baranda.

> **Pedro y Juan, ustedes instalan la baranda, ¿no?.**
> *Pedro and Juan, you guys install the banister. Right?*

Necesitamos poner los gabinetes de cocina.
We need to put in the kitchen cabinets.
Tenemos que poner los gabinetes de cocina.

> **Hoy ponemos los gabinetes de cocina.**
> *We are putting in the kitchen cabinets today.*

Ahora necesita meter los cajones.
Now you need to insert the drawers.
Tiene que meter los cajones en los gabinetes.

> **OK. Mete los cajones en los gabinetes.**
> *O.K. Put the drawers in the cabinets.*

Ojo. Necesitan alinear las tablas.
Watch it. You guys need to align the countertops.
Tiene que alinear las tablas.

> **Cuidado. Alinea las tablas.**
> *Careful. Align the countertops (you guys).*

Bueno. Necesitan poner los tornillos.
Good. You need to put in the screws.
Tienen que poner los tornillos.

> **Bueno. Ahora ustedes ponen los tornillos.**
> *Good. Now put in the screws.*

Sample Dialogue

You:	**Hoy necesitamos instalar las puertas.**
	We need to put in the doors today.
Tony	**Bueno. ¿Dónde empezamos?**
	Good. Where do we begin?
You:	**¿Por qué no *startean* con los exteriores?**
	Why don't you guys start with the exterior ones?
Tony:	**Está bien. Juan, sígueme.**
	O.K. Juan, follow me.
You:	**No. Juan necesita ayudarme hoy.**
	No, Juan needs to help me today.
Tony:	**¿Quién monta las bisagras?**
	Who is mounting the the hinges?
You:	**Pedro.**
	Pedro.

Tony: **¿Por qué Pedro?**
Why Pedro?

You: **Porque él necesita la práctica.**
Because he needs the practice.

RUFEANDO
(Roofing)

Necesitamos startear el rufo hoy.
We need to start the roof today.
Tenemos que startear el rufo hoy

> **Starteamos el rufo hoy.**
> *We are starting the roof today.*

Juan, necesita poner una linea de papel.
Juan, you need to put down a strip of tar paper.
Tiene que poner una linea de papel por favor.

> **Juan, pones una línea de papel, por favor?**
> *Juan, roll out a strip of tar paper.*

Necesita aplicar un poco de asfalto.
You need to apply a little tar.
Tiene que poner un poco de asfalto.

> **Aplica un poco de asfalto.**
> *Apply a little tar.*

Juan, necesita traerme la escalera.
Juan, you need to bring me the ladder.
Tiene que traerme la escalera.

> **Juan, trae la escalera.**
> *Juan, bring me the ladder.*

Ahora necesitan poner una linea de tejas.
Now you guys need to put on a row of shingles.
Tienen que poner una línea de tejas.

> **Ahora ponen una línea de tejas.**
> *Now put on a row of shingles. (You guys)*

Ojo. Necesita poner cubrejuntas aquí.
Don't forget—you need to put flashing here.
Ojo. Tiene que poner cubrejuntas aquí.

> **Ojo. Pon cubrejuntas aquí.**
> *Don't forget—put some flashing here.*

Necesita alinear cada fila de tejas.
You need to align each row of shingles.
Tiene que alinear cada fila de tejas.

> **Alinea cada fila de tejas.**
> *Align each row of shingles.*

Necesita superponer cada fila.
You need to overlap ("superimpose") each row.
Tiene que superponer cada fila.

> **Superpones cada fila.**
> *Overlap each row.*

Necesita usar dos clavos por teja.
You need to use two nails per shingle.
Tiene que usar dos clavos por teja.

> **Usa dos clavos por teja.**
> *Use two nails per shingle.*

Sample Dialogue

You:	**¿Cómo está el subrufo? ¿Listo?**
	How is the subroof? Is it ready?
Pablo:	**Sí. ¿Starteamos el rufo ahora?**
	Yes. Are we starting the roof now?
You:	**Claro. Ponga cubrejuntas en la chimenea.**
	You got it. Put flashing around the chimney.
Pablo:	**¿Por qué?**
	Why?
You:	**No queremos goteras.**
	We don't want any leaks.
Pablo:	**Está bien. ¿Cómo clavamos las tejas?**
	O.K. How are we nailing the shingles.
You:	**Usa dos clavos por teja, por favor.**
	Use two nails per shingle, please.
Pablo:	**¿De quién es éste martillo?**
	Who's hammer is this?
You:	**Es mío. Puede usarlo si quiere.**
	It's mine. You can use it if you want.
Pablo:	**Gracias. (Muchas gracias.)**
	Thanks. (Thanks a lot.)

EXTERIOR
(Exterior)

Necesitamos cubrir la estructura.
We need to cover the framing.
Tenemos que cubrir la estructura.

> **La cubrimos hoy.**
> *We are covering it today.*

Necesitan poner el entablado.
You guys need to put on the sheathing.
Juan y Carlos, tienen que poner el entablado.

Juan y Carlos, ustedes ponen el entablado.
Juan and Carlos, you guys put on the sheathing.

Ojo. Necesitan usar el triplay.
Look here. You guys need to use the plywood.
Tienen que usar el triplay.

> **Usan el triplay, por favor.**
> *Use plywood, please. (You guys)*

Ahora, necesitamos cubrirlo con papel.
Now we need to cover it with paper.
Ahora tenemos que cubrirlo con papel.

> **Ahora lo cubrimos con papel.**
> *Now we cover it with paper.*

Necesitan poner el forrado aquí.
You need to put siding on here.
Tienen que poner el forrado aquí.

> **Ustedes ponen el forrado en la fachada.**
> *You put the siding on the façade.*

Necesita cubrir el resto con alambre.
You need to cover the rest with wire.
Tiene que cubrir el resto con alambre.

> **Bueno. Ahora cubre el resto con alambre.**
> *Good. Now cover the rest with wire.*

Necesitan mezclar el estuco.
You guys need to mix the stucco.
Ustedes tienen que mezclar el estuco.

> **Pedro y José, ustedes mezclan el estuco.**
> *Pedro and José, you two mix the stucco.*

Necesita dompearlo en la carrilla.
You need to dump it into the wheelbarrow.
Tiene que dompearlo en la carrilla.

> **José, lo dompea en la carrilla.**
> *José, dump it into the wheelbarrow.*

Mire. Necesita allanarlo.
Watch. You need to trowel it.
Tiene que allanarlo.

> **Mire. Lo allana así.**
> *Watch. Trowel it like this.*

Sample Dialogue

You: **Hoy necesitan poner el entablado.**
      Today you guys need to put on the sheathing.

Pepe: **¿Quienes? ¿Todos nosotros?**
      Who? All of us?

You: **Usted, Carlos y Juan.**
      You, Carlos and Juan.

Pepe: **¿Y qué hace José?**
      And what is José doing?

You: **José necesita clavar el forrado.**
      José needs to nail on the siding.

Pepe: **Está bien. Vámonos.**
      O.K. Let's go.

You: **El triplay está allá.**
      The plywood is over there.

Pepe: **Carlos, Juan. Ayúdame a llevar el triplay.**
      Carlos. Juan. Help me bring (carry) the plywood.

You: **Cuidado. Está pesado.**
      Careful. It's heavy.

SHIROQUEANDO
(Sheetrocking)

Necesitamos poner (instalar) el shiroque.
We need to put up (install) the sheetrock.
Tenemos que poner (instalar) el shiroque.

> **Ahora, ponemos (instalamos) el shiroque.**
> *We're putting up (installing) the sheetrock now.*

Pedro, necesita medir y cortarlo.
Pedro, you need to measure and cut it.
Pedro, tiene que medirlo y cortarlo.

> **Pedro, lo mide y lo corta.**
> *Pedro, measure and cut it.*

Wáchelo. Necesitan clavarlo a los montantes.
Watch. You guys need to nail it to the studs.
Wáchelo. Tienen que clavarlo a los montantes, ok?

> **Wáchelo. Lo clavan a los montantes, ok?**
> *Watch. Nail it to the studs. (You guys)*

Ahora necesita aplicar pasta en las uniones.
Now you need to spread compound on the joints.
Ahora tiene que aplicar pasta en las uniones.

> **O.K. Ahora aplica pasta en las uniones.**
> *O.K. Spread taping compound on the joints.*

Necesita cubrir los clavos también.
You need to cover the nails too.
También tiene que cubrir los clavos.

> **También cubre los clavos [tornillos].**
> *Cover the nails [screws] too.*

174

Necesitamos aplicar teip y más pasta.
We need to apply tape and more compound.
Tenemos que aplicar teip y más pasta.

> **Entonces aplicamos teip y más pasta.**
> *Then we apply the tape and more compound.*

Despues necesita usar la paleta para alisarlo.
Later you need to smooth it with a taping trowel.
Despues tiene que usar la paleta para alisarlo.

> **Despues usted usa la paleta para alisarlo.**
> *Later you use the taping trowel to smooth it out.*

Necesitan lijar las uniones.
You guys need to sand the joints.
Tienen que lijar las uniones.

> **Ahora lijan las uniones, ¿O.K.?**
> *Now you guys sand the joints. O.K.?*

Ojo. Necesitan limpiar las paredes.
Heads up. You guys need to clean the walls.
Ojo. Tienen que limpiar las paredes.

> **Bueno. Ahora limpian las paredes.**
> *Good. Now clean the walls.*

Sample Dialogue

You: **Juan, shiroquea el living [la sala] hoy.**
Juan, sheetrock the living room today.
Juan: **¿Tenemos suficientes paneles?**
Do we have enough sheetrock?
You: **Sí, aquí y en el garage.**
Yes, here and in the garage.

Juan:	¿Dónde está mi naife? No está aquí.
	Where is my knife? It isn't here.
You:	Aquí está el mío. Puede usarlo.
	Here's mine. You can use it.
Juan:	Gracias. ¿Puede ayudarme Pedro?
	Thanks. Can Pedro help me?
You:	Sí, él puede poner el teip cuando venga.
	Yes, he can tape when he gets here.
Juan:	¿A qué hora terminamos hoy?
	What time are we quitting today?
You:	A las cinco en punto. Tengo una cita.
	At five sharp. I have an appointment.

ELÉCTRICO
(Electrical)

Necesitan instalar las cajas [enchufes].
You guys need to install the outlets.
Tienen que instalar los enchufes.

> Ustedes instalan las cajas [enchufes].
> *You guys install the electrical outlets now.*

Juan, necesita taladrar los montantes.
Juan, you need to drill the studs.
Juan, tiene que taladrar los montantes.

> Juan, taladra los montantes.
> *Juan, you drill the studs.*

Pablo y Carlos, necesitan puchar el conducto.
Pablo and Carlos, you need to push the conduit.
Pablo y Carlos, tienen que puchar el conducto.

> Pablo y Carlos, ustedes puchan el conducto.
> *Pablo and Carlos, push the conduit.*

Necesita jalarlo, Arturo.
You need to pull it, Arturo.
Lo tiene que jalar, Arturo.

> **Jálalo, Arturo.**
> *Arturo, you pull it.*

Necesitamos jalar el alambre [el cable].
We need to pull the wire.
Tenemos que jalar el alambre [el cable].

> **Ahora jalamos el alambre [el cable].**
> *Now we pull the wire.*

Necesita cortar los cables.
You need to cut (or trim) the wires.
Tiene que cortar los cables.

> **Usted corta los cables.**
> *You cut (or trim) the wires.*

Bueno. Necesita conectarlos a los suiches.
Good. You need to attach them to the switches.
Bueno. Tiene que conectarlos a los suiches.

> **Bueno. Los conecta a los suiches por favor.**
> *Good. Connect them to the switches.*

Juan, necesita flipear el suiche [interruptor].
Juan, you need to flip the switch.
Juan, tiene que flipear el suiche.

> **Juan, flipea el suiche, por favor.**
> *Juan, flip the switch, please.*

177

Necesita apagar el suiche de circuito.
You need to shut off the breaker switch.
Tiene que apagar el suiche de circuito.

> **Usted apaga el suiche de circuito.**
> *Shut off the breaker switch.*

Sample Dialogue

You: **Empezamos con el eléctrico hoy.**
We are starting on the electrical (wiring) today.

Pepe: **¿Dónde ésta el conducto flexible?**
Where's the flex conduit?

You: **Está en el dining.**
It's in the dining room.

Pepe: **Bueno. ¿Dónde empiezo?**
O.K. Where do I start?

You: **¿Por qué no empieza en la cocina?**
Why don't you start in the kitchen?

Pepe: **Está bien. ¿Y Juan?**
Gotcha. And what about Juan?

You: **Quiero que él instale las cajas.**
I want him to install the outlets.

Pepe: **Él no sabe como hacerlo.**
He doesn't know how to do it.

You: **Pues, es hora de que aprenda.**
Well, it's time he learns.

PLOMERÍA
(Plumbing)

Necesitamos completar la cocina hoy.
We need to finish the kitchen today.
Tenemos que completar la cocina hoy.

> **Completamos la cocina hoy.**
> *We're finishing the kitchen today.*

178

Necesita instalar el sink, drenaje, y trampa.
You need to install the sink, drain and trap.
Juan tiene que instalar el sink, drenaje y trampa.

> **Juan, usted instala el sink, drenaje y trampa.**
> *Juan, you install the sink, drain and trap.*

Bueno. Ahora usted necesita poner los grifos.
Good. Now you need to put in the faucets.
Bueno. Ahora usted tiene que instalar los grifos.

> **Bueno. Ahora usted instala los grifos.**
> *Good. Now you put in [install] the faucets.*

Necesitan instalar los artefactos de baño.
You guys need to install the bathroom fixtures.
Ustedes tienen que instalar los artefactos de baño.

> **José y Carlos, ustedes dos instalan los artefactos del baño.**
> *José and Carlos, you two install the bathroom fixtures.*

Necesitan poner la bañera aquí y el toilet allá.
You guys need to put the tub here and the toilet over there.
Tiene que poner la bañera aquí y el toilet allá.

> **Ustedes ponen la bañera aquí y el toilet allá.**
> *Put the tub here and the toilet over there.*

Necesita instalar la llave de mezcla en la ducha.
You need to install the mixing valve in the shower.
José, tiene que instalar la llave de mezcla en la ducha.

> **José, usted instala la llave de mezcla en la ducha ¿O.K.?**
> *José, install the mixing valve in the shower.*

179

Necesita usar una conexión en "T" aquí.
You need to use a "T" fitting here.
Tiene que usar una conexión en "T"

> **Para eso, usa una conexión en "T".**
> *Use a "T" fitting for that.*

Necesita medir, cortar y roscar un tubo de drenaje.
You need to measure, cut and thread a drainpipe.
Tiene que medir, cortar y roscar un tubo de drenaje

> **Ahora usted mide, corta y rosca un tubo de drenaje.**
> *Now please measure, cut and thread a drainpipe.*

Sample Dialogue

You: **José, necesitamos completar el sink.**
José, we need to finish the sink.

José: **Pongo el drenaje y trampa ahorita.**
I am putting in the drain and trap right now.

You: **Y los grifos, ¿Dónde éstan?**
And the faucets—where are they?

José: **En la caja encima del gabinete.**
In the box on top of the cabinet.

You: **Bueno. ¿Está bien todo allá abajo?**
Good. Everything going O.K. down there?

José: **No puedo unir el drenaje y la trampa.**
I can't connect the drain to the trap.

You: **Corta el tubo un poco.**
Shorten (cut) the pipe a little.

José: **Y, ¿las roscas?**
And what about the threads?

You: **Necesita roscarlo de nuevo.**
You need to rethread it.

SECTION III

Take a Break

Whew! Time for a well-deserved break. Many of you are feeling pretty overwhelmed, and may be wondering if now would be a good time to drop this class and enroll in something useful like *Underwater Basket Weaving*, or *Eastern Mysticism for Fun and Profit*. If any of you *can* still say you are fully with the program, either we have discovered a great teaching method (*a big maybe*) or you have a natural knack for learning foreign languages *(more possible)*, or you are completely delusional and wouldn't recognize reality if it jumped up and bit you in the posterior *(just as possible)*. Whatever you're feeling at this point, don't make any hasty decisions without reading what I am about to tell you. Trust me, it's important.

So what was with that Section II? I mean, *verbos* up the *wahzoo*, one right after the other, *no?* I know what some of you are thinking: *"What kind of a sadist is this guy? He lures me in nice and easy with Section I, and just when I think I'm getting somewhere, he comes at me like some kind of runaway verb pile-driver. What's next—pulling off my fingernails with a rusty pair of pliers?!"* O.K., a little explanation may be in order. In case you missed it, the point was to show you *how to learn verbs*, not to force you to learn every one of *those* verbs before moving on. If you got the concept of the four forms, and are making flash cards or practice lists to memorize the verbs and other words *you need most* for what *you* want to say, then you are still doing fine. Each of those verbs in Section II will still be there when you need them.

As for the question of what comes next, here's the good news—you're pretty much there. *Say, what?* Seriously, dudes (and dudettes, to be politically correct) I'm not just pulling your chain. Take Sections I and II, add in the Quickies, and you have what you need for basic jobsite communication. That being said, you may not be feeling anyplace close to being there, wherever *there* is. Yeah, you have learned a lot of really useful Spanish words, and that's cool. You can even put some of them together, and communicate a few things that seem to be understood. But it sure doesn't feel natural. You have to work at it each time you want to say anything--and you still can't seem to follow much of that the native Spanish speakers are saying, especially when they are talking to each other (they do talk fast, don't they?). So, you're feeling a little frustrated (if you scored high on the *anal* test, make that feeling downright *depressed!*). Fair enough.

Don't feel like you are alone here, or that you are just not cut out for learning a language. Everyone hits this wall of feeling frustrated or inadequate, and I can tell you from experience that most of it is mental. We all get impatient when things we really want don't come easy or fast. Here's the thing. Most people give up on language programs, not because of bad program content, but because the program failed to tell them what to expect, mentally and emotionally, as they follow the steps and move through the materials. Everyone starts with high hopes and expectations, learns some of the basics, and then starts to doubt themselves when it doesn't all suddenly *click*. Isn't there supposed to be some magical point where speaking Spanish feels just like speaking English?

Learning a skill like a second language is not one of those things where one day you aren't bilingual, and the next day you are. Think of it as a rafting trip down a river—you know where the river starts and ends, but it is the journey, the "getting there" that presents the challenges. There will be stretches where the river moves smoothly, and all you have to do is go with the flow (sorta like Section I of this book), and there are likely to be some rather hairy white water rapids (Section II, anybody?). So far, so good with the analogy. But, think about it—there are also those occasional pools where the water doesn't seem to be moving at all, and your raft just drifts aimlessly around, going nowhere in particular. Yeah, there actually is current there, and you will eventually move on downstream, but it sure doesn't seem like it at the time. You will experience this as well in learning Spanish (or maybe you already have?), times when you just don't seem to be getting anywhere, times when you begin to wonder if you are ever going to get to the end of your language journey.

The important thing about hitting one of these "still water" periods is deciding what you are going to do about it. You can give up, thinking "Well, it was fun while it lasted, but I guess this is the end of the line for me. I'm just not making any more progress." Or, you can start paddling like mad, trying to somehow defy nature and move faster than the current will allow—leaving yourself too exhausted to handle the next set of rapids, which are likely to appear when you least expect. The moral of this story is that impatience, my friends, leads directly to frustration. When we are frustrated, we stop thinking straight and start to subconsciously psych ourselves out. Here are some of the ways in which we allow impatience and frustration to misdirect our efforts. See if any of these fit with the driftwood you may have collected and are dragging along like an anchor.

Loss of Focus

Stop a minute and think. Do you even *remember* what the original goal was? It wasn't to become magically bilingual and apply for an overseas embassy assignment as a translator with the U.S. Diplomatic Corps—no, it was to learn to *communicate* better with Spanish-speaking workers on the job site. This is a process of moving from pointing and gesturing to learning some key Spanish words for things, and from there to some progressive stages of *Spanglish*. By that I mean a lot of English and pointing to start, with a few Spanish words mixed in as you learn them, and then slowly replacing the English with more and more Spanish as your vocabulary grows. Remember our telling you that it doesn't have to always be exactly the right word, or pronounced exactly the right way—that close is good, and not-so-close will still generally get you by? Well, that was then, and this is now. As you have learned more and more Spanish, you may have allowed yourself to become bogged down in the "Am I saying this right?" trap, and started choking. If so, you have lost focus. Your progress will pick up speed again when you relax, stop worrying, and refocus on the goal of learning to *communicate (even if that means communicating ugly for a while)*, instead of on *learning to immediately speak fluent Spanish.*

Temptation

This is the trap that snares all you gung-ho cowboys out there. Yeah, you know who you are. To hell with all that advice about taking things one step at a time, you're gonna knock this thing off in thirty days or less. Memorize it all and be done with it. You can't resist the *temptation* to just keep going, without giving your brain time to fully digest, file and store each new piece of information. I gotta tell ya that it just don't work that way. The brain, and I mean *everybody's* brain, *without exception*, has two kinds of memory—short-term and long-term. Thank God for small favors. I mean, there are a ton of things I need to remember (i.e., *memorize, "commit to memory"*) for brief periods of time, like where I just put my car keys, or that I have a dentist's appointment tomorrow. I need them in the ol' memory tub right now, but I sure don't want to still be remembering them a week, a month, or a year from now. Then there are other things, like language skills and my wife's birthday, that I need in there permanently. You with me so far? *Bueno.*

Everything first goes into short-term memory, and things only move from there to long-term storage when the brain figures out that it is actually worth keeping. (It is generally based on how often you use the info. The more time in and out of the file, the more the brain is convinced it is worth keeping. Info that doesn't get used, gets booted.) Also, the short-term memory part of the brain doesn't have all that much storage space—it is designed for temporary storage only, and the more you overload it with too much info all at once, the faster it tosses info into the trash bin instead of moving it into the permanent files. So, if you are serious about learning to communicate in Spanish, get rid of the temptation to push things too fast. Memorize one, or at most a few words at a time, starting with the ones you use most in your particular trade. Then use them a lot. The more you use them, the quicker your brain will move them to long-term memory. Once the new language file is set up in long-term storage, each new Spanish word you learn and use will be automatically moved to where it logically fits in this new file. So, *chill*, slow down a little, and you can stop worrying about whether you are getting early Alzheimers. It's not your *memory*, it's your *method!*

Fear

None of us like to admit to this one (at least not publicly), but the little gremlin is always around, isn't he? So, what are you afraid of? Some of you will say fear of not being able to learn this stuff—fear of just not getting it. Others will say fear of looking and feeling foolish in trying any of it. Can we all agree that the real fear is that it isn't going to work for you, that the native Spanish speakers are never going to really understand you? Isn't that really it, bottom line? My only response to you is, *HELLO-O-O-O??!! They couldn't understand you to begin with! Duh.* Remember? Your English wasn't cutting it? That's why you are trying to learn some Spanish in the first place? Come on, guys—every construction-related Spanish word you learn and use is one more thing they probably *do understand*. No, you are not going to hit the bull's-eye every time, especially when first starting, but at least you're now somewhere on the target, and that is progress.

Let me give you an example here. You say, "Where is my hammer?", and everyone gives you the usual blank, clueless stare. However, if you change one single word and say, "Where is my *martillo*?", at least now they know you are saying *something* about a *hammer*, right? They may not know exactly what your issue is with a hammer, but when you show your hands are empty and start looking around while saying *martillo*, someone will put two and two together and figure it out. One more word, *"Dónde* is my *martillo?"*, or even, "My *martillo, dónde?"* and I guarantee they will understand your problem immediately. Yeah, I know, some things get more complicated than this example, but my point is valid. Your fears are basically groundless—every word you learn and use is one more thing you *can* communicate, at least some of the time, and that leaves you better off than you were before. And it only gets better as you keep learning and practicing.

Lack of Motivation

We need to have a little talk about two guys named "Moe"—MO-tivation, and MO-mentum. Whenever you're trying to learn a new skill (any skill) these two guys are gonna show up and make your life interesting. They remind me of one of those giant, gorilla-sized tag teams in the WWF—one look at them, and I know whose side *I'm* on. I may be a half-bubble off plumb, but I ain't *completely* nuts! In fighting to learn a new skill, I want these two *hombres* in my corner, and you should too. Especially that MO-tivation dude, cuz' without him, ol' MO-mentum is just not himself. On his own, he can be kind of a *wuss*—pretty much a no-show when the match is on the line.

So, here's the thing about the main Moe—motivation. It's something you either got or don't got. It's not anything I or anybody else can give you, no matter how much rah-rah I try to shovel at you. Motivation exists inside of *you,* if it exists at all. Any of you remember that old bit of folksy wisdom, "You can lead a horse to water, but you can't make him drink"? Hits the nail right on the head. If the horse is thirsty enough, he will be *motivated* to drink. If not, there's nothing you can do—including holding his head under water until he drowns. The thirst/motivation-to-drink thing just isn't there for him.

O.K., mini-quiz time (yeah, I know I promised no tests, but this one only has three questions, so it doesn't really count). You need to imagine yourself in each of the following situations, and pick the response that comes closest to what you think you would actually do under the circumstances.

1. You run out of gas in your new boat, 20 miles off the coast. It's getting cold and dark, and there's a storm brewing on the horizon. The only help for miles around is a Mexican fishing boat out of La Paz. Which would you do?

a. Grab your five-gallon gas can, jump overboard, and take your chances swimming to shore through shark-infested waters in search of an all-night gas station,

   or

b. Do your best to flag down the fishing boat, and try whatever *Spanglish* you can remember in order to get a little help.

2. As the last man on earth, you find yourself stranded on a tropical island with the *last woman on earth*—a gorgeous South American bombshell who doesn't speak a word of English (Who said learning Spanish can't be fun?). Would you

a. Take an immediate vow of celibacy (for all you non-Catholics, that means *No Sex!*) and spend the rest

187

of your life contemplating your navel, completely ignoring the beautiful señorita?

or

b. Brush off your rusty *Spanglish*, work up your nerve, and try to win the sweet little *muchacha's* heart?

3. While you are on vacation in Guadalajara, your hot, spicy lunch catches up with you (or maybe they were right about not drinking the water?). Anyway, you find yourself sitting on the john in a public restroom, doing your thing, when you notice that there is no toilet paper in your stall. Would you

a. Try to make do with your socks or "tidy whities", and then make a run for it when nobody is looking (leaving the offending articles behind)?

or

b. Pound on the partition, and use whatever *Spanglish* you can remember to get some paper from the guy in the stall next to you?

The quiz is a pretty much a no-brainer, right? Everybody gets an A grade by picking *b*. So, what's the point? Well, your choices say a lot about *motivation,* now don't they? You have all just confessed that, given the right situations, you would be *highly motivated* to babble away in Spanish/*Spanglish*, without fear of sounding foolish, or worrying about any "am I saying this right" crap. Bless you, my children, confession is good for the soul. You have now admitted to yourselves that you *could do this* if you really, *really* wanted to. So put all the rest of the excuses aside, and ask yourself, *Without someone holding a gun to my head, how much do I really want to learn to communicate in Spanish?* If you are motivated, you will keep working at it, and the more you learn and *use*, the more momentum (the other half of the tag team) you will pick up. If your answer to yourself is that you really aren't that motivated, then consider getting your money's worth out of this book by using it as a doorstop.

And My Point Is . . . ?

With the construction-related vocabulary (both Spanish and easy *Spanglish* terms), memory hints, shortcuts, sample sentences, and the smart way of learning verbs, you actually do have most of the information and tools you need to communicate with Spanish-speaking workers on the job site. Moving the information from the pages of this book into your own long-term memory and productive use is a different matter altogether. Turning all this into an actual, usable *skill* requires time, commitment, and prac-tice—*especially practice*. Even when you are fully moti-vated and committed, your learning curve will not always ascend at a steep angle; be prepared to gain ground, and then "plateau" or coast for periods of time before gaining more ground (remember the river?). Whenever you feel yourself coasting when you think you should be growing, review this section. Is it that you have lost focus, or are you letting some fears sneak in the back door? Are you losing your desire and motivation, or, as is generally the case, is it just that your brain needs to take a break in order to get a better handle on what you have already learned? Don't beat yourself up, or get discouraged and want to quit. Even though the river sometimes rushes at 90 miles per hour, and other times doesn't seem to even be moving, all the water mysteriously gets to its final desti-nation, and so will you.

End of pep talk, sermon, psychoanalysis, whatever you want to call it. Let's move on to some extra-credit stuff you might find interesting and useful.

SECTION IV

Lesson 14: If Not Now, When?

Everything we have covered so far is in the *present tense*,
real time, online, live, happening *NOW!* So, what if we
need to talk about something that is *going to happen*, or
something that has *already happened?* We promised you
that we would cover future and past tenses, didn't we?
Did you think (or hope) we would forget? Not a chance.
Are you kidding me—pass up a golden opportunity to tor-
ture you with more verbs? This is more fun than pulling
wings off flies. Verbs to me are like porno to the rest of
you—*give me more, more, I'm still not satisfied!*

But, enough about me. Where were we? Oh, yes . . .
future and past tenses. Why now? I mean, didn't I tell
you a few pages back that you were pretty much already
there with what you needed to know for communicating in
Spanish/*Spanglish*? Well, the plain, unvarnished truth is
that you don't absolutely need future and past tenses for
basic communication. The trick is to use the present
tense, which you know something about *(presuming you
have been paying attention)*, and tack on a time reference
out of Quickies 4 or Quickies 5, like *yesterday, last week,
tomorrow, next week,* etc. This will tip off whoever you
are talking to that you are really talking about sometime
other than the immediate here and now.

So, how does this work? *Well, I'm glad you asked—*
actually, you are already pretty used to hearing some of
this from those native Spanish-speaking co-workers of
yours who are trying to learn English. Do you notice little
grammatical inconsistencies like *"I do that yesterday", "I
do that later", "I go there tomorrow",* and so on? They are
doing exactly what I am talking about—using the present
tense of whatever verb, along with a time reference in the
future or past. You generally understand what they mean,

don't you? In fact, it gets to the point where you almost stop noticing it—you know English isn't their native language, and you're just happy you can understand them, bad grammar and all. Using this same method will at least get you by in Spanish, same as it does for them in English. Grammatically, it is about as *ugly* as the worst blind date you've ever had, but *like you care?* Let's look at a few examples:

When you say:	**Lo hago <u>ayer</u>.**
Actual translation:	I *do* that yesterday.
What is understood:	I *did* that yesterday.
When you say:	**Trabajamos <u>el domingo pasado</u>.**
Actual translation:	We *work* last Sunday ("this past Sunday").
What is understood:	We *worked* last Sunday.
When you say:	**Juan va <u>hoy en la tarde</u>.**
Actual translation:	Juan *goes* this afternoon ("today in the afternoon").
What is understood:	Juan *is going to go (will go)* this afternoon.
When you say:	**Necesita más madera <u>mañana</u>.**
Actual translation:	You *need* more lumber tomorrow.
What is understood:	You *will need (are going to need)* more lumber tomorrow.
When you say:	**Hablo con usted <u>más tarde</u>.**

Actual translation: I *speak* with you later
                        ("more tardy").

What is understood: I *will speak (am going to speak)*
                        with you later.

Frankly, there are people who never learn anything
more than the present tense of a foreign language, and
they manage to get by using this sneaky little trick. You
could too, allowing you to skip the next two lessons (future
tense and past tense), but I don't recommend it, because
your Spanish-speaking co-workers will be using these
tenses, and you might like to eventually know exactly what
they are saying. For example, when you say to Jorge,
"Necesita hacer eso", and he answers, *"Lo hacía"*, what did
he just say?

a. *"O.K., I'll do it."*

b. *"I already did it."*

c. *"In your dreams, Gringo."*

Remember, communication is a two-way street, and the
more Spanish you learn, the better you will begin to understand the native speakers.

What I do recommend is that you use what we have
just given you until you feel comfortable with the future
and past tenses. Neither of them is particularly difficult
to learn, especially where you already know and are regularly using the same verbs in the present tense, but learning to comfortably shift time zones with your verbs will
take a fair amount of time and practice. If you try to push
it too fast, you are going to fall right back into the "Am I
saying this right?" trap, and start choking on your verbs
again. At least test-drive the following two lessons, so you
will know what they will offer you when you are ready to
seriously tackle them.

Even when I use the future or past tense of a verb, I still add in the appropriate time reference word *(tomorrow, last Wednesday,* etc.). While it might not be absolutely necessary, it does two things for me. It keeps me using those words (remember, *no use 'em, you lose 'em*), and it gives me an easy way out if I get a sudden brain-cramp in the middle of a sentence, and can't remember the future (or past) tense of the verb I'm using. I just default to the present tense. I know I will be understood. I don't need to worry about adding the time reference, since I put that in out of habit, anyway. You might keep this in mind—works for me!

Nosotros ***necesitábamos***   necesit + **ábamos**
(We *needed* or *needed to*)

Ustedes, ellos, ellas ***necesitaban***   necesit + **aban**
(You guys/they *needed* or *needed to*)

 Ah, caught that one, did you? Yeah, the *yo, usted, and el/ella* forms are all the same—no misprint. In the past tense, you sometimes have to use a pronoun, to clear up any confusion. Are you talking about yourself, or about the person you are talking *to*, or about someone else?

Once you get used to it, though, it does make this tense even easier—for –ar verbs, you only have to memorize three endings, **aba, ábamos, aban**.

Putting this into our visual graphic form for easier memorization, we are looking at the following:

necesit**aba**	necesit**ábamos**
necesit**aba**	necesit**aban**

And the really sweet thing about this is that it works for all the –ar verbs you already know and use. You are not going to find any of those pesky spelling and pronunciation changes in the stem that you saw in some present tense verbs (like *contar* going to *cuento, cuenta,* etc.). You can trust the infinitives in the past tense—just drop the –ar, and add the above endings as needed. See what I mean about almost no irregular verbs in this tense? Makes it worth learning.

Moving right along here, we get to the –er and –ir verbs, which we can deal with together, because they are basically the same in the past tense—another freebie that the past offers those of us who have been killing off brain cells with the *cerveza* and other products of "better living through chemistry". (Yeah, sure, you never touch *any* of that other stuff—save it for the judge.) Let's use hacer, *to do*, for our example, because it's the verb you are probably going to need and use the most in the past tense.

Yo **hacía**   hac + **ía**
(I *did*)

Usted, el, ella **hacía**   hac + **ía**
(You, he, she *did*)

Nosotros **hacíamos**   hac + **íamos**
(We *did*)

Ustedes, ellos/ellas **hacían**   hac + **ían**
(You guys/they *did*)

I'm sure you again noticed that the *yo, usted,* and *el/ella* are the same, consistent with the –ar pattern we just covered. So, one more time, you only have to memorize three basic endings: **ía, íamos, ían.** Again, putting it into our visual, hacer in the past tense is

hac**ía**	hac**íamos**
hac**ía**	hac**ían**

My own little mental shortcut for deciding which of these two ending types to use on which verbs is to remember that Spanish verbs are separated into -ar and -er/-ir categories. For the past tense, I connect aba with -ar verbs because the endings both *begin* with the letter a, and in like fqshion, I connect ía with the others because it begins with the letter i like –ir verbs and is pronounced like the English letter e , which covers the -er verbs for me as well. Make sense? Yeah, well, don't worry about it—my shrink has some serious concerns about the way I think as well.

The few irregular verbs in this past tense are -er/-ir verbs, so once you memorize them, you can go back to trusting the infinitive for all the others, like we just explained for -ar verbs. The two main irregular verbs, *ser (to be)* and *ir (to go)*, are two annoying verbs that seem to like being different in most tenses. You will recall from the Dirty Dozen lesson that both of these are irregular in the present, and I don't even want to try to explain just how utterly *bizarre* they are in the preterite. Anyway, here they are in our past tense:

Ser
to be

era	eramos
era	eran

Ir
to go

iba	íbamos
iba	iban

O.K., another (hopefully) helpful hint here. You will have to memorize these two, but the problem is sometimes remembering which one goes with which infinitive. My method is to connect **e**ra with s**e**r, because it seems logical for the past tense ending of an -er verb to begin with e, and to connect iba with ir, to keep the two "i" words together.

Of the 200 most important verbs in the Spanish language, these two verbs are the only ones irregular in the imperfect past tense. As a means of comparison, of these same 200 verbs, over 50 of them are irregular in the preterite past tense. I rest my case.

Lesson 17: Mixing It Up

Now that you have added future and past to your language toolbox, we are going to give you a couple of practice exercises. (*Easy there*, big fella! When I promised you no *tests*, I never said anything about *exercises*.) The first will give you some realistic job site conversations, mixing all three tenses (present, future, past) as they might normally occur, along with the English translation.

To practice your recognition of tenses, cover up the English with a sheet of paper, and see how you do in understanding what is said. You can then peek at the translation to test your comprehension. The more you practice this exercise, the quicker your brain will begin to naturally shift between tenses.

Exercise 1

— **Juan, *necesita* instalar el *cilín* en el *livin* hoy.**

— *Juan, you need to install the ceiling in the living room today.* [present tense]

— **Pero, ya lo *hacía*.**

— *But I already did it.* [past tense]

— **¿Cuándo *hacía* eso?**

— *When did you do that?* [past tense]

— **Ayer en la tarde.**

— *Yesterday afternoon.*

— **Ah. No lo *sabía*. ¿Y los dormitorios?**

— *Oh. I didn't know that. And the bedrooms?* [past tense]

— **Voy a hacerlos hoy.**

— *I'm going to do them today.* [future]

— **Bueno.** ¿*Tenemos* **suficiente** *shiroque* **[plancha de yeso]?**

— *Good. Do we have enough sheetrock (plasterboard)?* [present]

— **Ellos** *van a traer* **más hoy en la mañana.**

— *They are going to bring more this morning.* [future]

— **Si no** *vienen,* **¿por qué no** *trabaja* **con Pedro en el eléctrico?**

— *If they don't come, why don't you work with Pedro on the wiring?* [present]

— *Está* **bien, pero no** *sé* **nada del sistema eléctrico.**

— *O.K., but I don't know anything about electrical systems.* [present]

— **¿No** *hacía* **usted algo de eléctrico en la otra casa?**

— *Didn't you do some electrical in the other house?* [past]

— **No. Yo no.**

— *No. Not me.*

— **No** *importa.* **Pedro** *es* **un experto. Usted** *puede aprender* **de él.**

— *It doesn't matter. Pedro is an expert. You can learn from him.* [present]

— **¿Cuándo** *vamos a completar* **la plomería en la cocina y los baños?**

— *When are we going to finish the plumbing in the kitchen and baths?* [future]

— **Dentro de poco. Ahorita** *necesitamos* **completar los cilins y el eléctrico.**

— *Pretty soon. Right now we need to finish the ceilings and the electrical.* [present]

— **¿A qué hora** *vamos a terminar* **hoy?**

— *What time are we going to quit today?* [future]

— A las tres. El jefe no *permite* horas extraordinarias.

— *At three o'clock. The boss doesn't allow any overtime.* [present]

— Pero *teníamos* tres días de lluvia. No *vamos a completar* ésta casa a tiempo.

— *But we had three days of rain. We aren't going to finish this house on time.* [past, future]

— Ya lo *sé*, pero así *es* como *es*.

— *Tell me something I don't already know, but that's the way it is.* [present]

You probably noticed that speaking Spanish is a lot like speaking English—everyone mixes up their tenses according to what they are trying to say. This is why it helps to understand a little bit of the future and past tenses— yeah, you can get by with just the present tense when you are talking, but understanding what the other guy is saying is sometimes the hardest part.

Now, for the next little exercise, we are going to reverse the English and Spanish sides of exercise 1, so that you can practice getting the right verb form in Spanish—we are even going to give you the verb itself and the tense, to help you out a little. Again, use a sheet of paper to write down what you think the verb form should be. (Yeah, you *could* just write your answers in the book, *Einstein,* but then you wouldn't be able to do it more than once, now would you?) When you finish, you can check your answers against the Spanish sentences in exercise 1.

Exercise 2

— Juan, you *need to* install the ceiling in the living room today. [present]

— **Juan, *(necesitar)* instalar el** cilin **en el** livin **hoy.**

— But, I already *did* it. [past]

— **Pero, ya lo *(hacer).***

— When *did you do* that? [past]

— **¿Cuándo *(hacer)* eso?**

— Yesterday afternoon.

— **Ayer en la tarde.**

— Oh. I *didn't know* that. How about the bedrooms? [past]

— **Ah. No lo *(saber)*. ¿Y los dormitorios?**

— *I'm going to* do them today. [future]

— ***(Ir a)* hacerlos hoy.**

— Good. *Do we have* enough sheetrock? [present]

— **Bueno. ¿*(tener)* suficiente** shiroque**?**

— They *are going to* bring more this morning. [future]

— **Ellos *(ir a)* llevar más hoy en la mañana.**

— If they *don't come*, why don't *you work* with Pedro on the wiring? [present]

— **Si no *(venir)*, ¿por qué no *(trabajar)* con Pedro en el eléctrico?**

— O.K., but I *don't know* anything about electrical. [present]

— **Está bien, pero no *(saber)* nada del eléctrico.**

— *Didn't you do* some of the electrical in the other house? [past]

— **¿No *(hacer)* usted algun eléctrico en la otra casa?**

— No. Not me.

— **No. Yo no.**

— *It's not important.* Pedro *is* an expert. You *can learn* from him. [present]

— **No _(importar)_. Pedro _(ser)_ un experto. Usted _(poder)_ aprender de él.**

— When *are we going to* finish the plumbing in the kitchen and baths? [future]

— **¿Cuándo _(ir a)_ completar los** cilíns **y los baños?**

— Pretty soon. Right now *we need to* finish the ceilings and the electrical. [present]

— **Dentro de poco. Ahorita _(necesitar)_ completar los cilins y el eléctrico.**

— What time are we going to quit today? [future]

— **¿A qué hora _(ir a)_ terminar hoy?**

— At three o'clock. The boss doesn't allow any overtime. [present]

— **A las tres. El jefe no _(permitir)_ horas extraordinarias.**

— But we had three days of rain. We're not going to finish this house on time. [past, future]

— **Pero _(tener)_ tres días de lluvia. No _(ir a)_ completar ésta casa a tiempo.**

— Yeah, I know, but that's just the way it is. [present]

— **Ya lo _(saber)_, pero así _(ser)_ como _(ser)_.**

A little tougher when you try it from English to Spanish, right? That's why it requires practice, practice, *practice* before it starts coming naturally. However, if you are following our recommendation of the flash cards with the graphic format, it should come a little easier. What you want to do is get a good mental picture of the four zones on the graphic—when you need to say something, identify the *who* you want to talk about, and mentally focus on only that zone of the graphic. If you can do this, your only remaining choice is whether you want to say it in the present, future or past.

Let's again use our favorite verb, *necesitar,* as an example. When I want the *who* to be myself, I mentally see only the top left of the graphic, because I know that is my place—the **Yo**.

present

necesito

future

voy a necesitar

past

necesitaba

When I want the *who* to be you, he or she, I simply change my mental focus to the bottom left zone of the graphics I have already memorized:

present

necesita

future

va a necesitar

past

necesitaba

When the *who* is we, I shift my mental picture to the top right of the graphics, ignoring everything else:

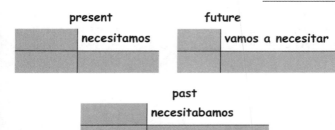

present

necesitamos

future

vamos a necesitar

past

necesitabamos

Although I think you already get the point, let's go ahead and finish. When the *we* is the plural you (*you guys*) or they *(those guys, them)*:

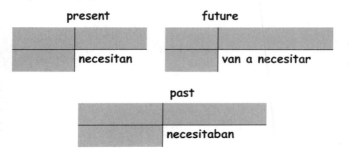

present

necesitan

future

van a necesitar

past

necesitaban

Once you get the hang of exercises 1 and 2, you may want to make up some of your own sentences, based on what kinds of things you are dying to talk about or say at work. You can cater them to your specialty, or to those things you are having the hardest time communicating. Work those sentences until you have them memorized cold, and then use them as often as you possibly can. Surprisingly enough, our brains pick up not only the things we learn and use, but also the *patterns* of speech we use. Once you know how to say certain things, and want to say other things of a similar nature, your brain will give you a *no sweat* signal, and put the new sentence together for you. The reason for practicing whole sentences or thoughts, rather than simply memorizing vocabulary, is because language is based on *whole patterns of speech*, not just single words.

SECTION V

Lesson 18: Making Nice

All work and no play makes for a dull world, so I'm sure you would like to learn a few things that don't have to do with foundations, framing, or sanitary traps, right?. Well, now that you are getting the hang of *palavering* a bit in the *ol' español*, we thought we might help you polish your social skills. You will find native Spanish speakers to be *uncommonly* polite, at least judging by how we act. They not only greet you and ask how you are, they have this *weird craving* to shake hands all the time! It doesn't even matter if your right hand is already occupied, they're perfectly willing to shake your *left* hand instead. They'll shake your hand when either you or they arrive, and want to shake again whenever one of you decides to leave. But this isn't the worst of it—when they really get to know you, they will use the handshake as a good grip for pulling you into a *hug*. Yeah, I'm talking about grown men hugging—without a winning touchdown being scored, a few too many *cervezas*, or any other halfway decent alibi. Go figure.

Now, before I get myself in trouble here, I'm (not putting down their culture or anything. I mean, it's not as bad as the French and Italians who want to kiss you on both cheeks (and get your mind out of the *gutter*). The only reason for mentioning all this is that I don't want you to be surprised, or to think that there are any *closet affections* involved. It's just a part of how they were raised, and there is nothing wrong with being polite—even with strangers. We could probably use a little help in this department (especially people in New York City, who make a special effort to avoid any eye contact, let alone anything physical like offering to shake hands). So, having angered a few million people so far, including whole countries in addition to the Big Apple (which only *thinks* it's a country), now might be a good time to move on. The following is a good short list of some "make nice" vocabulary you should learn.

MAMA'S FAVORITES

por favor
[pohr fah-VOHR]

Please   Literally means *as a favor (to me)*, which is what it's all about. When we say please, it's generally because we want someone to do something which is going to benefit us more than them, right?

gracias
[GRAH-see-ahs]

Thank you   One you probably already know (it's pretty basic), but you need to practice using it a lot.

de nada
[deh NAH-dah]

You're welcome

Literally means *for nothing*, which certainly makes more sense than our English way of saying it. I mean, you're welcome to what . . . my paycheck, my car, my wife, *what?*

HOW'S IT GOIN'?

hola
[OH-lah]

Hello   Not too difficult to pick up—the word starts with the same letter in both languages. Just remember that the letter h is always silent in Spanish—and, no, I don't know why they put it in all those words if you are never supposed to use it.

buenos días
[BWEHN-ohs DEE-ahs]

Good morning

> A couple of things to watch out for here. First, día (day) is one of those weird masculine words which ends in the letter a, so it's buenos días. Second, even though día means *day*, buenos días means *good morning*, not good day. It's only used before noon.

buenas tardes
[BWEHN-ahs TAHR-dehs]

Good afternoon

> Remember the cognate *tarde/tardy* means *late,* so it makes sense to use *tarde* for afternoon, as it is later in the day.

buenas noches
[BWEHN-ahs NO-chehs]

Good evening/night

> Again, not too hard to connect the two "n" words, noche and night. But *please* remember that it is noches, and not nachos. You can't wish someone a "good tortilla chips with melted cheese".

¿cómo está?
[KOH-moh ehs-TAH]

How are you?

> If you are asking more than one person, make it plural, ¿cómo están?, or ¿cómo están todos? (how're y'all doin'?)

¿qué tal?
[KEH tahl]

How are you?

> Generally used as a greeting among friends, it

215

is *idiomatic*, meaning that it is understood in the language, even though translating the words themselves *(what such?)* into another language ends up not making any sense.

bien
[bee-EHN]

Fine   Literally means *well*, as in "I'm doing well." And always remember to be polite by following it with *gracias*.

así-así   mas o menos
[ah-SEE ah SEE]   *[mahs oh meh-nohs]*

So-so   *Así-así* is old *Spanglish*. Use **mas o menos** if you want to sound more as a native speaker. With this response you probably don't need the *gracias*. Why thank someone for reminding you that you're having a lousy day?

¿Y usted?
[ee oo-STEHD]

And you?   This is the typical polite response after you have said *bien* or *así-así*. They asked you how you are, so you need to return the favor and ask them how they are.

bueno
[BWEHN-oh]

Great, or *glad to hear it*
When you ask someone how they are, and they answer *bien*, this response will let them know you are happy for them.

lo siento
[loh see-EHN-toh]

I'm sorry to hear that
Good response to así-así. Literally means "I feel it", sorta like those touchy-feely Holly-

wood types who say things like "I feel your pain".

GLAD T' MEETCHA

¿cómo se llama?
[KOH-moh say YAH-mah]

What's your name?

> We covered llamarse in the Dirty Dozen, but here's a reminder—in Spanish, they don't ask, *What's your name?* They ask, *How do you call yourself?*

Me llamo . . .
[may YAH-moh]

My name is . . . (I am called . . .)

> This is how you answer when asked, *"¿Cómo se llama?* You say *Me llamo Homer Hammerhead*, or whatever you call yourself these days. If you draw a complete blank on llamarse, you can get by with *Soy Homer Hammerhead*— "I'm Homer".

mucho gusto
[MOO-choh GOOS-toh]

Pleased to meet you.

> Literally, "with great pleasure", this is the easiest way to acknowledge an introduction to someone. It's the short way of saying the very proper *Tengo mucho gusto en conocerlo*—"I am very pleased to meet you".

encantado
[ehn-cahn-TAH-doh]

Charmed This is another way of acknowledging an introduction. Sounds like some English snob saying "Charmed, I'm sure". The reason I mention it is, if you are being introduced to a

Spanish-speaking woman, you will score more points with *encantado* than *mucho gusto*.

SAY GOODNIGHT, GRACIE

adiós
[ah-dee-OHS]

Goodbye   I'm sure you have all watched enough cowboy flicks to already know this one, so I don't need to explain it.

hasta la vista
[AHS-tah lah VEES-tah]

Later, dude.   Literally means until we see each other again. I think you might recognize this one from Bruce Willis' memorable line in one of those *Die Hard* classics of his. You can also say *hasta luego*—"until later". Same dif.

es hora de despedirme
[ehs OHR-ah deh dehs-peh-DEER-meh]

It's time for me to go

Sounds like a bad line out of a Barry Manilow song, doesn't it? It is one common (and corny) way of saying that you're leaving. Goes well with *encantado*—"charmed" for those trying to score points with the opposite sex or. . . never mind.

ya me voy
[yah meh VOY]

I'm outta here

Literally, "I'm going now". Probably the easiest way of telling folks you're not sticking around.

que tenga buen día
[kay TEHN-gah bwehn DEE-ah]

Have a nice day

> Pure *Spanglish*. Someone just took that over-
> used English expression and translated it.
> You won't find this much outside of the ol'
> U.S. of A. (thank God for small favors!).

que lo pase bien
[kay loh PAH-seh bee-EHN]

May all go well with you

> Yeah, like you are going to bother memorizing
> this. It's the Spanish way of saying "have a
> nice day", and if you use it you will get a lot of
> smiles and respect, because it is *sooooo* edu-
> cated and *polite*.

These little gems will help you get by in the social
aspects of your job, without embarrassing yourself too
much. However, if you are the type who gets bored saying
the same things over and over, or the type who wants to
sound cool around your fellow workers, then you might
want to consider a few of the following options:

¿cómo se encuentra?
[KOH-moh say ehn-KWEHN-trah]

How are things treating you?

> An option when you are tired of saying ¿cómo
> está? Generally used with friends and people
> you know.

¿cómo le va?
[KOH-moh leh VAH]

How's it going?

> Another alternative, slightly more *slangy*
> than ¿cómo se encuentra? Use with friends.

¿qué pasa?
[KEH PAH-sah]

What's going on?

> One more step down on the formality scale, definitely slang, good for the job site.

¿qué hubo?
[KEH OO-boh]

What happened?

> We're getting down to real street talk here—is the past of ¿que pasa?, most times said as **quihubo** *[KyOO-boh]* or **quihúbole** *[KyOO-boh-leh]*. Their English equivalents could be *Wass-happening* or *Wattup*.

¿qué onda, primo?
[KAY OHN-dah PREE-moh]

What up, cuz?

> Doesn't go any lower than this on the slang scale—if you use it, you will get some real belly laughs from native Spanish speakers, as well as a few questions about where you learned this one. Not typical Gringo turf. This is street corner, barrio talk (if you need help with this, try renting a couple of Cheech and Chong movies—that should get you down to the right level). Not your classroom Spanish.

Lesson 19: Taking Care of Business

I'm guessing that some of you out there in readerland must be contractors or managers who would like some vocabulary to help you with the business side of working with Spanish-speaking employees. Nobody likes paperwork and dealing with employment issues, and it gets a whole lot hairier when there is a language as well as cultural barrier. Some of the following should help you with what you need to do. We will even give you the phonetic pronunciation, in case you had to jump ahead to this lesson out of desperation. We covered some of the vocabulary you need in the last lesson, so we are going to build on that rather than repeating things like "what's your name?"

¿Habla inglés?
[AH-blah een-GLEHS]
Do you speak English?

¿Busca trabajo?
[BOOS-kah trah-BAH-ho]
Are you looking for work?

No tengo nada ahora. Lo siento.
[noh TEHN-goh NAH-dah ah-OHR-ah. loh SYEHN-toh]
I don't have anything now. Sorry.

¿Qué tipo de trabajo hace?
[KEH TEE-poh deh trah-BAH-ho AH-seh]
What kind of work do you do?

¿Tiene experiencia? ¿Dónde?
[tee-EHN-eh ehx-pehr-ee-EHN-cee-ah. DOHN-deh]
Do you have experience? Where?

Necesita completar ésta *aplicación.*
[nay-see-SEE-tah kohm-pleh-TAHR EHS-tah ah-pleh-kah-SYON]
You need to fill out this application.

[The proper Spanish word is **solicitud** *(sohl-ee-see-TOOD)* but most people will understand the *Spanglish* term *aplicación* for employment application. The word exists in Spanish, but is used for the application of paint, etc.]

Este número de teléfono, ¿es de su casa o para mensajes?

[EHS-teh NOO-mehr-oh deh teh-LEH-foh-noh, ehs deh soo KAH-sah oh pah-rah mehn-SAH-hehs]
Is this your home phone, or a message number?

¿Hay alguien allí que habla inglés?

[ay AHL-gee-ehn ah-YEE kay AH-blah een-GLEHS]
Is there someone there who speaks English?

Necesita completar ésta forma para impuestos federales.

[neh-seh-SEE-tah kohm-pleh-TAHR EHS-tah for-mah pah-rah ehm-PWEHS-tohs feh-dehr-AHL-ehs]
You must fill out this federal tax form.

Y ésta de impuestos estatales.

[ee EHS-teh deh ehm-PWEHS-tohs ehs-tah-TAH-lehs]
And this one for state taxes.

También ésta forma I-9 del gobierno.

[tahm-bee-EHN EHS-tah FOHR-mah dehl goh-BYEHR-noh]
Also, this government I-9 form.

Necesita mostrarme la identificación que indica en la forma.

[neh-seh-SEE-tah mohs-TRAHR-meh lah ee-dehn-tee-fee-kah-SYON keh een-DEE-kah ehn lah FOHR-mah]
You must show me the actual I.D. that you list on the form.

Necesita mostrar una de columna A . . .

[nay-say-SEE-tah mohs-TRAHR oo-nah deh kohl-OOM-nah AH]
You need to show one from column A . . .

O una de cada una de B y C.
[oh OON-ah deh KAH-dah OON-ah deh BEH ee SEH]
Or one each from B and C.

Sin la identificación adecuada, no puedo emplearlo.
[seen lah ee-dehn-tee-fee-kah-SYON ah-deh-KWAH-dah, noh PWEH-doh ehm-pleh-AHR-loh.]
Without proper I.D., I can't hire you.

Lo siento. Es la ley.
[loh see-EHN-toh. ehs lah lay]
I'm sorry. It's the law.

No quiero problemas con *la Migra*.
[noh kee-HER-oh proh-BLEH-mahs kohn lah MEE-grah]
I don't want any problems with the I.N.S.

¿Tiene su credencial de la *unión* (sindicato)?
[tee-EHN-eh soo kreh-den-SEE-al deh lah oon-YOHN (seen-dee-KAH-toh)]
Do you have your union card?

[The more proper Spanish word for labor union is *sindicato*, but in the U.S. that sounds like the "sindicate"—the Mafia—so we give a new *Spanglish* meaning to the word *unión*.]

¿Puedo verla por favor?
[PWEH-doh VEHR-loh por fah-VOHR]
Can I see it, please?

¿Lo manda la *unión*?
[loh MAHN-dah lah oon-YOHN]
Did the union send you?

¿Puedo ver la hoja?
[PWEH-doh VEHR lah OH-hah]
Can I see the referral slip?

¿Tiene sus propias herramientas de mano?
[tee-EHN-eh soos PROH-pee-ahs HER-rah-MYEN-tahs deh MAH-noh]
Do you have your own tools?

Si no, entonces no puedo emplearlo.
[see NOH, ehn-TOHN-says noh PWEH-doh ehm-pleh-AHR-loh]
If not, I can't use you.

Voy a pagarle _____ dólares por hora.
[voy ah pah-GAHR-leh __ DOH-lahr-ehs pohr OH-rah]
I'll pay you _____ dollars per hour.

. . . menos descuentos por impuestos (beneficios,cuota de la unión).
[MEH-nohs dehs-KWEHN-tohs pohr eem-PWES-tohs (beh-neh-FEE-see-ohs, KWOH-tah deh lah oon-YOHN).
. . . less deductions for taxes (benefits, union dues).

Pago al final (de cada día, de la semana, de cada otra semana, del mes)
[PAH-go ahl fee-NAHL (deh KAH-dah DEE-ah, deh lah seh-MAHN-ah, deh KAH-dah OH-trah seh-MAHN-ah, dehl MEHS]
I pay at the end of (each day, the week, every other week, the month).

El día de pago es cada (otro) viernes (sábado, domingo, etc.)
[ehl DEE-ah deh PAH-go ehs KAH-dah oh-troh VYEHR-ness,(SAH-bah-do, doh-MEEN-goh]
Payday is every (other) Friday (Saturday, Sunday, etc.).

¿Puede trabajar mañana?
[PWEH-deh trah-bah-HAR mah-NYAH-nah]
Can you work tomorrow?

¿Tiene licencia de conducir?
[tee-EHN-eh lee-SEHN-see-ah deh kohn-doo-SEER]
Do you have a driver's license?

¿Está enfermo? Necesita regresar a casa.

[ehs-TAH en-FEHR-moh. neh-seh-SEE-tah reh-greh-SAHR ah KAH-sah]
Are you sick? You need to go home.

¿Tiene herida? ¡Vaya al doctor/la clínica ahora mismo!

[tee-EHN-eh ehr-EE-dah. VAH-yah ahl dohk-TOHR/lah KLEE-nee-kah ah-OHR-ah MEES-moh]
Did you hurt yourself? Go to the doctor/clinic immediately!

No alcohol ni drogas en el área de trabajo—incluso cerveza.

[noh ahl-koh-OHL nee DROH-gahs ehn ehl AH-ree-ah deh trah-BAH-ho—een-KLOO-soh sehr-VEHS-ah]
No alcohol or drugs on the job—including beer.

The above will at least give you a start, and, as you work your way through the book, you will find new ways of saying what you need. Employees are, if anything, highly creative in the kinds of problems they bring up, and it would be impossible to give you the perfect sentence to cover all of them. Tell me about it, this is the stuff I actually do for a living. Surprise, surprise. I'm not writing this from a room with rubber walls down at the local funny-farm. I have a real job (if you consider what human resources people do as actual *work*, that is). While you are learning some of this stuff, you will need some support. Most of the time, your current Spanish-speaking workers will explain to the new guy what it is you expect of him, as well as things like paydays, lunch breaks, and any no-nos you may have. If you have someone who is bilingual, give him a raise and use him as your interpreter until you are confident in your own Spanish abilities.

Lesson 20: Cover Yer Ears!

We're not children here, and I think we understand that language on the job site can get pretty spicy (that's *picante* in Spanish, by the way). The first and most important point we want to make here is that no one in his or her right mind should ever try swearing in a foreign language—it can only get you in trouble. Depending on how they are used, "potty mouth" words in Spanish, like in English, can have multiple meanings, some humorous, some harmless, and some downright dangerous! Our purpose for introducing some of these more commonly used words is not for you to ever attempt to use them yourself. However, since you *are* going to hear them, sometimes frequently, we thought you should at least learn to recognize them. Many dictionaries don't include them, so where else are you going to find out? If you are seriously offended by swearing, or for any other reason would rather not know *everything* that is being said, feel free to skip the remainder of this section.

Cabrón
Equivalent of calling someone a *sonofabitch*, a *bastard,* or maybe an *asshole*. Be very careful here—this is very insulting and its use may get someone a hammer up alongside their head.

Carajo
There is no exact translation, but it is used as an exclamation of disgust, surprise or frustration—like the English use of ***damn!, dammit!, shit!***, etc.

Gringo
This is a term used to describe Anglos, especially those from the U.S. Can be used in a friendly or joking way, which is pretty harmless, but if someone calls you a *pinche gringo* (see *pinche*, below), you can pretty much guess that you are being insulted.

Pendejo
Another one which will generally get someone pretty riled up. Equivalent of calling someone a *coward*, or an *idiot*, in a very insulting way. (Literally translated, it's a pubic hair, so I think you get the picture.) Can lead to bloodletting.

Pinche
This is an adjective which is placed in front of a noun, like *pinche cabrón*, for example. Generally means *low-class, worthless, low-life, scum bastard,* etc. When used to describe objects (*pinche clavo, pinche martillo,* etc.) it is completely harmless, but used to describe a person it is always meant as an insult.

WARNING!

**DO NOT ENTER!
RED ALERT!
BEWARE! NO TRESPASSING!**

There is one other series of words in Spanish which carry warnings from OSHA, NIOSH (the National Institute of Safety and Health), the Surgeon General, and NSPBH-GLS (the National Society for the Prevention of Bodily Harm to Gringos Learning Spanish), to name just a few. These warnings cover <u>any</u> words which begin with:

ching-.

These words, both nouns and verb, represent various forms of the "F" word in Spanish. There are like a gazillion different expressions in Spanish which use various forms of the base word, from something as blunt as "f---you!" to many others covering almost any possible thing that could happen in life—funny, sad, frustrating, insulting, and downright dangerous. We are hereby putting you on notice that, with one possible exception, you should not only *never* attempt to use any of these yourself, you should also do your best to go stone cold deaf when you hear them used by anyone else. Any reaction will leave you either embarrassed or in deep, *deep* tapioca!

Now for the one reasonably safe exception. In English, we have a whole bunch of words (actually non-words) which we use when we don't know the right name for something, right? Words like *whatchamacallit, doohickey, thingamabob, whoozit,* and so on. Well, a very commonly used word among Spanish-speaking workers for this purpose is *chingadera.* If you use this word while pointing at, demonstrating, or explaining something, you will probably get a few smiles or laughs from your co-workers.

But, that's all she wrote, folks. End of subject. Other than this one sole exception, do not attempt to swim in this pool—in fact, don't even stick your toe in the water! While trying to keep the tone of this book as light and fun as possible for learning purposes, I am dead serious about this warning, and *dead* ain't a bad way of describing how you may end up if you don't take the teacher's advice on this one.

SECTION VI

Lesson 21: And That's an Order!

Honest, I was only going to cover three verb tenses, present, future, past, but my editor (a native Spanish speaker, but what does *he* know) beat me--two out of three--in online arm wrestling. As a reward, he insisted I at least say *something* about command forms in Spanish. So, here goes nothing. In English, we don't really have any special forms of verbs for commands (the so-called *imperative* for all you anal types who look this stuff up in grammar books)—we just use the infinitive without the *to* in front, and say it real loud. Like, for example, Go!, Stop!, Help!, Do it!, *Beat me! Hurt me! Make me write bad checks! ooooh!* (Jeez, what movie *was* that in—Valley Girl?) Anyway, you get the picture. This method wouldn't work in Spanish, where verbs are made up of stems and seeds— oops, minor Freudian slip there—stems and *endings.* Something has to be done to the endings to change present tense forms from factual statements like "You do it" (*indicative*) to commands like "Do it!" (*imperative*). They actually came up with a pretty sneaky and *easy* way of doing this. We'll take it in steps:

1. We pretty much only use the command form in giving direction to someone else, either a single person or a group, right? I mean, if you give orders to yourself, you might have a little problem. *(HELLO-O-O! I'm not schizophrenic, and neither am I!)* We know that present tense –ar verbs give us endings of **a** and **an** (hablar = habla and hablan) when we mean *you* in the singular and plural. We have also learned that –er/-ir verbs give us endings of **e** and **en** (hacer = hace and hacen, and abrir = abre and abren). So, to make commands, what is easier than to switch these two sets of endings, using **e** and **en** for –ar verbs, and **a** and **an** for –er/-ir verbs? When anyone knows what **trabajar** normally sounds like, they are going to notice the difference:

Indicative	Imperative
You **work** *fast*	**Work** *fast!*
trah-BAH-**hah**	trah-BAH-**heh**
trah-BAH-**hahn**	trah-BAH-**hehn**
You eat	*Eat!*
KOH-**meh**	KOH-**mah**
KOH-**mehn**	KOH-**mahn**

To native Spanish speakers, this comes as natural as eating jalapeños—their ears are tuned in to these little differences almost from birth. For Gringos like us, it takes a lot more concentration and practice. The point is, however, that we recognize the stem, so we kinda know what they are saying even if it sounds a little funny.

2. Now, here's where it gets interesting. Even though we are switching the *third person singular and plural endings*, we are going to add them onto the *first person singular stem*—the "yo" form. We take the "yo" form of the verb, drop the **o** ending, and add the command ending instead. Here are a couple of examples:

Hablar
(to Speak)

Indicative
First person   habl**o**   Yo habl**o** claro
                                      (*I speak clearly.*)

Imperative
Third person:

Singular	hab**le**	Hable claro
		(Speak clearly!) [you]
Plural	hab**len**	Hablen claro
		(Speak clearly!) [you guys]

Barrer
(to Sweep)

Indicative

First person	barr**o**	Barro el piso
		(I sweep the floor)

Imperative
Third person:

Singular	barr**a**	Barra el piso
		(Sweep the floor!) [you]
Plural	barr**an**	Barran el piso.
		(Sweep the floor!) [you guys]

3. "But wait", I hear you cry, "isn't first person singular where a lot of verbs are *irregular?*" You got it! However, it isn't as bad as you may think. The two irregularities are adding a **g** in front of the o ending, like in ha**go**, *I do,* or adding a **y** after the o like in es**toy**, *I am*. All you have to remember is that anything *in front of* the o stays in, while anything *after* the o gets removed with the o, in order to add the command endings. Confused? O.K, let's look at a few examples:

Hacer
(to Do)

Indicative

First person	ha**go**	Hago el trabajo
		(I do /am doing the work)

Imperative
Third person:

Singular	ha**ga**	Ha**ga** el trabajo
		(Do the work!) [you]
Plural	ha**gan**	Ha**gan** el trabajo
		(Do the work!) [you guys]

Other common verbs like hacer which add the **g** in the first person are tener-*to have (tengo),* venir-*to come (vengo),* poner-*to put (pongo),* and decir-*to say (digo).*

Estar
(to Be)

Indicative

First person	est**oy**	Estoy aquí a las ocho
		(I am here at 8 o'clock)

Imperative
Third person:

Singular	est**é**	Esté aquí a las ocho
		(Be here at 8) [you]
Plural	est**én**	Estén aquí a las ocho
		(Be here at 8) [you guys]

Another common verb like estar which adds the **y** in the first person is dar-*to give (doy).*

4. And finally, we come to our two pain-in-the-butt verbs, *ser* and *ir,* which are irregular any chance they get. In this case, however, it really isn't their fault. The key to using command forms is that the listener has to recognize the verb stem in order to know what verb you are using, whether you are speaking in the indicative or the imperative. *Ser* is another one of the **oy** verbs in the first person indicative, but if we drop the **oy** we are left with nothing but the letter s. Since it is an –er verb, adding **a** and **an** would give us unrecognizable commands of Sa! and

San! that don't leave any hint of what the actual verb might be. So, instead we have:

Ser
(to Be)

Indicative

First person   **soy**   Soy honesto
                                      (I am honest)

Imperative

Third person:

    Singular   **sea**   Sea honesto
                                    (Be honest) [you]

    Plural   **sean**   Sean honestos
                                    (Be honest) [you guys]

The verb *ir* has similar problems. If you remember our Dirty Dozen lesson, *ir* is not only another **oy** verb in the first person indicative, but somehow also slips in the letter *v*—*voy*. If we dropped the **oy** and added an **a** and **an**, the command form would be exactly the same as the indicative— *va* and *van*. So, why not add a few letters to the command form? I mean, the verb is so screwed up already, how much more damage could we do? You can decide for yourself—here is the command form of *ir:*

Ir
(to Go)

Indicative

First person   **voy**   Voy a lonche
                                      (I go to lunch)

Imperative

Third person:

    Singular   **vaya**   Vaya a lonche
                                    (Go to lunch) [you]

| Plural | **vayan** | Vayan a lonche |
| | | *(Go to lunch) [you guys]* |

O.K., so now you finally understand all those Clint Eastwood spaghetti westerns, where he has finished killing all the nogoodniks, and all the peasants gather around him in what's left of the town square, wearing what look like straw hats and white pajamas. The town leader steps forward and says, "Gracias, señor. *Vaya con Dios!* " You were hearing the *imperative* of the verb *ir- to go*-- "Go with God!", and didn't even know it. I'm telling you, for the education you're getting here, I should be charging you more!

5. As long as we are on the subject of the verb *ir*, we might mention a few special uses of the command form involving *we* instead of *you/you guys*. The most often used *we* command is "Let's go!" which like all forms of the verb *ir* is a little irregular. The indicative is *vamos (we go, we are going)*, and the imperative is close—**vámonos!** *[VAH-moh-nohs] (Let's go!)*. Good word to know for going to lunch, leaving at the end of the day, and getting out of the bar before the fight starts! There may be other times when you want to include yourself in a "command" you are giving to others, and to do that, follow the pattern you just learned for third person commands—using **emos** for -ar verbs and **amos** for –er/-ir verbs. Sort of like this:

Beber (to drink)
> **¡Bebamos unas cervezas!**
> *(Let's drink some beers!)*

Levantar (to lift, to raise)
> **¡Levantemos esto juntos!**
> *(Let's lift this together!)*

Venir (to come)
> **¡Vengamos temprano mañana!**
> *(Let's all come early tomorrow!)*

This last part is probably beyond what you want to learn about command forms, and I can't say I blame you.

You might be better off sticking to the third person commands, with the exception of *vamonos*, which does get used a lot.

In most things we say on the job, we have a choice of using the indicative with a *please* and *thank you,* or the imperative and shine the social niceties. I mean, in English I can say, "Would you please hand me that box of nails" *(indicative)*, or "Gimme that box of nails" *(imperative)*, and nobody is going to see any difference. The Latino culture is generally more polite (see the last lesson), but when mixed with our way of doing and saying things, begins also to lose a little of the distinction between the polite indicative and the imperative in day-to-day work situations. The command form probably gets more use here than in most Latin American countries, because of the English way of speaking.

Now for the big question, to see if any of you have been staying awake. After working through the rules for commands, anyone out there have any bells or whistles go off in the ol' brain? Remember my saying over and over not to sweat trying to get things exactly right—that close was good? You now know why. If you blow it and put an –ar ending on an –er verb or vice versa, you will be not only understood, but often *technically* correct! It just means you may have used the *imperative* instead of the *indicative* to get your point across. You might not sound as polite as you intended, but you still communicated effectively. I just love it when a plan comes together!

Lesson 22: Odds and Ends

Yeah, you could see it coming. I just couldn't wrap this up without throwing out a couple of more *verbs!* In my own defense, I'm honestly not trying one last shot at torturing you. It's just that there are a couple of verbs which are so unique that I didn't want to put them in the basic verb lessons, for fear of confusing you any more than I already have. In fact, I would be glad to skip them completely, except they are used so much that you should at least know what they are.

hay *[aye]*   *there is, there are* [present]

habrá *[ahr-AH]*   *there will be* [future]

había *[ah-BEE-ah]*   *there was, there were* [past]

That's all there is to this verb—no infinitive needed, no *yo* or *nosotros* forms, and the singular and plural are both the same. This has to be the easiest verb in the Spanish language. It is used only for general, or *impersonal* statements and questions, which means it cannot be used when talking about a *specific person* like usted, el, ella, ustedes, ellos, or ellas. How is it used, then? Here are a few examples:

Present Tense

¿Cuántos montantes *hay* en la pila?
How many studs *are there* in the pile?

***Hay* once.**
There are eleven.

***Hay* mucho trabajo en el verano.**
There is a lot of work in the summer.

Hay menos en el invierno.
There is less in the winter.

Hay mucha gente sin trabajar.
There are a lot of people without work.

No *hay* tiempo para eso.
There isn't any time to do that.

¿*Hay* clavos en esa caja?
Are there any nails in that box?

No, no *hay*.
No, *there aren't*.

Future Tense

Habrá mas trabajo la proxima semana.
There will be more work next week.

Habrá una entrega al mediodía.
There will be a delivery at noon.

Past Tense

Había una gotera en la unión.
There was a leak in the joint.

¿No *había* más tejas en el garage?
Weren't there more shingles in the garage?

No, no *había* nada allí.
No, *there was* nothing there.

Pretty simple, huh? However, because in the present tense it sounds like the English *I* and *eye*, it takes a little getting used to. Since you will be hearing (and hopefully *using*) it a lot, it will begin to click at some point—you will suddenly realize that when Juan says *"no hay"*, he means *there isn't any*. He's not saying "Not me" or "I'm blind".

gustar *to like [someone or something]*

This is one of the *trickiest* verbs to learn in Spanish. If you remember, back in the lesson on The Dirty Dozen we gave you *llamarse*, with a quick rundown on *reflexive* verbs—those with the *-se* added onto the end of the infinitive. Ring any bells? The ones where the action of the verb turns back on the subject of the sentence—"*I call myself* Homer" instead of "My name is Homer". When you look at the infinitive, *gustarse* looks like one of those, doesn't it? Well, it isn't exactly, and here's why.

Using *llamarse*, when you say *me llamo . . .* you mean "I call myself . . .", right? So, if *gustarse* worked the same way, saying *me gusto . . .* would mean "I like myself", not that you like *someone* or *something*. Well, then, just how do we say something like "I like enchiladas"? Here is how the verb *gustar* works:

Me gusta.   *I like it.*

Me gustan.   *I like **them**, I like **those**.*

Le gusta.   *You, he, she likes it.*

Le gustan.   *You, he, she likes **them**, or likes **those**.*

Nos gusta.   *We like it.*

Nos gustan.   *We like **them**, or **those**.*

Les gusta.   *You guys or they like it.*

Les gustan.   *You guys or they like **them**, or **those**.*

Seems a little confusing, if not downright weird, doesn't it? You can see that there are only two forms to the verb, the third person singular and plural (**gusta, gustan**). This is because in Spanish there is no way to say *I like, you like, they like,* etc. Instead, people say things like *that pleases (or is pleasing to) me, those are pleasing to us, they are pleasing to them,* etc. It is completely bassackwards from our English sentence structure. You know how much I hate grammar, but I am going to have to throw some in here so that you can get this concept.

When I make a statement in English such as "I like enchiladas", the subject of the sentence is "I"—I'm talking about myself, something *I* like. The verb is *like,* and *enchiladas* are the *object* of the sentence, in this case the object of my affections, right? Whenever you want to say this same thing in Spanish, using *gustarse,* you have to turn the sentence completely around. In Spanish, *enchiladas* is the subject of the sentence (after all, we're talking about enchiladas, right?), and *I* becomes the object instead— *Enchiladas are pleasing **to me**.* Can you see where this leads? In English the subject *(I)* was singular, while the object *(enchiladas)* was plural. Turning it around, suddenly the subject *(enchiladas)* is plural and the object *(yours truly)* is singular. Therefore, in Spanish, we get

Me gust**an** las enchiladas

where the verb has to be plural, because the subject is *enchiladas* and not *me.* If I say

Nos gust**a** el color
(We like the color)

the verb is singular because the subject *color* is singular— the plural *we* refers to the objects, not the subject.

We are not going to go into the grimy details of direct and indirect object pronouns, because they are way, *way* beyond our *object* of teaching basic job site communication skills. However, to use *gustar*, you might want to simply memorize the following:

Indirect Object Pronouns

me *[meh]*   to me

le *[leh]*   to you, to him, to her

nos *[nohs]*   to us

les *[lehs]*   to you guys, to them

Don't feel bad if you find yourself struggling with the uses of *gustar*. It takes lots of practice, and lots of making mistakes, before anyone gets it completely right. There are a small handful of other verbs which are like *gustar*, but none that you can't live without. Concentrate on learning how to use this one, and if you ever find you need any of the others, you will know how they work by reminding yourself, "This one is just like *gustar*".

Appendix A: Verb Forms

aflojar *(to loosen)*

Present Tense		Past Tense	
aflojo	aflojamos	aflojaba	aflojabamos
afloja	aflojan	aflojaba	aflojaban

Future Tense	
voy a aflojar	vamos a aflojar
va a aflojar	van a aflojar

alisar *(to plane, to smooth)*

aliso	alisamos	alisaba	alisabamos
alisa	alisan	alisaba	alisaban

voy a alisar	vamos a alisar
va a alisar	van a alisar

allanar *(to smooth, to trowel)*

allano	allanamos	allanaba	allanabamos
allana	allanan	allanaba	allanaban

voy a allanar	vamos a allanar
va a allanar	van a allanar

apagar *(to turn off)*

apago	apagamos	apagaba	apagabamos
apaga	apagan	apagaba	apagaban

voy a apagar	vamos a apagar
va a apagar	van a apagar

aplicar *(to apply)*

aplico	aplicamos	aplicaba	aplicabamos
aplica	aplican	aplicaba	aplicaban

voy a aplicar	vamos a aplicar
va a aplicar	van a aplicar

apretar (ie) *(to tighten, to squeeze)*

aprieto	apretamos	apretaba	apretabamos
aprieta	aprietan	apretaba	apretaban

voy a apretar	vamos a apretar
va a apretar	van a apretar

chequear (to check) Spanglish

chequeo	*chequeamos*	*chequeaba*	*chequeabamos*
chequea	*chequean*	*chequeaba*	*chequeaban*

voy a *chequear*	vamos a *chequear*
va a *chequear*	van a *chequear*

clavar *(to nail)*

clavo	clavamos		clavaba	clavabamos
clava	clavan		clavaba	clavaban

	voy a clavar	vamos a clavar
	va a clavar	van a clavar

conectar *(to connect)*

conecto	conectamos		conectaba	conectabamos
conecta	conectan		conectaba	conectaban

	voy a conectar	vamos a conectar
	va a conectar	van a conectar

construir *(to construct, to build)*

construyo	construimos		construía	construíamos
construye	construyen		construía	construían

	voy a construir	vamos a construir
	va a construir	van a construir

cortar *(to cut)*

corto	cortamos		cortaba	cortabamos
corta	cortan		cortaba	cortaban

	voy a cortar	vamos a cortar
	va a cortar	van a cortar

cuadrar *(to "square")*

cuadro	cuadramos		cuadraba	cuadrabamos
cuadra	cuadran		cuadraba	cuadraban

	voy a cuadrar	vamos a cuadrar
	va a cuadrar	van a cuadrar

derramar *(to pour, to spill)*

derramo	derramamos		derramaba	derramabamos
derrama	derraman		derramaba	derramaban

	voy a derramar	vamos a derramar
	va a derramar	van a derramar

doblar *(to bend, to double)*

doblo	doblamos		doblaba	doblabamos
dobla	doblan		doblaba	doblaban

	voy a doblar	vamos a doblar
	va a doblar	van a doblar

dompear (to dump) Spanglish

dompeo	dompeamos		dompeaba	dompeabamos
dompea	dompean		dompeaba	dompeaban

	voy a *dompear*	vamos a *dompear*
	va a *dompear*	van a *dompear*

elevar *(to elevate, to raise)*

elevo	elevamos		elevaba	elevábamos
eleva	elevan		elevaba	elevaban

	voy a elevar	vamos a elevar
	va a elevar	van a elevar

estar (estoy) *(to be)*

estoy	estamos		estaba	estábamos
está	están		estaba	estaban

	voy a estar	vamos a estar
	va a estar	van a estar

excavar *(to dig, to excavate)*

excavo	excavamos		excavaba	excavábamos
excava	excavan		excavaba	excavaban

	voy a excavar	vamos a excavar
	va a excavar	van a excavar

flipear (to flip) Spanglish

flipeo	flipeamos		flipeaba	flipeabamos
flipea	flipean		flipeaba	flipeaban

	voy a flipear	vamos a flipear
	va a flipear	van a flipear

fremear (to frame) Spanglish

fremeo	*fremeamos*	*fremeaba*	*fremeábamos*
fremea	*fremean*	*fremeaba*	*fremeaban*

voy a *fremear*	vamos a *fremear*
va a *fremear*	van a *fremear*

hacer (hago) *(to do, to make)*

hago	hacemos	hacía	hacíamos
hace	hacen	hacía	hacían

voy a hacer	vamos a hacer
va a hacer	van a hacer

igualar *(to equal, to even up)*

igualo	igualamos	igualaba	igualábamos
iguala	igualan	igualaba	igualaban

voy a igualar	vamos a igualar
va a igualar	van a igualar

instalar *(to install)*

instalo	instalamos	instalaba	instalábamos
instala	instalan	instalaba	instalaban

voy a instalar	vamos a instalar
va a instalar	van a instalar

jalar *(to pull, to haul)*

jalo	jalamos		jalaba	jalábamos
jala	jalan		jalaba	jalaban

	voy a jalar	vamos a jalar
	va a jalar	van a jalar

lijar *(to sand)*

lijo	lijamos		lijaba	lijábamos
lija	lijan		lijaba	lijaban

	voy a lijar	vamos a lijar
	va a lijar	van a lijar

limpiar *(to clean, to wipe)*

limpio	limpiamos		limpiaba	limpiábamos
limpia	limpian		limpiaba	limpiaban

	voy a limpiar	vamos a limpiar
	va a limpiar	van a limpiar

medir (i) *(to measure)*

mido	medimos		medía	medíamos
mide	miden		medía	medían

	voy a medir	vamos a medir
	va a medir	van a medir

meter *(to put in[to], to insert)*

meto	metemos		metía	metíamos
mete	meten		metía	metían

	voy a meter	vamos a meter
	va a meter	van a meter

mojar *(to wet, to moisten, to dampen)*

mojo	mojamos		mojaba	mojábamos
moja	mojan		mojaba	mojaban

	voy a mojar	vamos a mojar
	va a mojar	van a mojar

necesitar *(to need [to], to necessitate)*

necesito	necesitamos		necesitaba	necesitábamos
necesita	necesitan		necesitaba	necesitaban

	voy a necesitar	vamos a necesitar
	va a necesitar	van a necesitar

nivelar *(to level, to make even)*

nivelo	nivelamos		nivelaba	nivelábamos
nivela	nivelan		nivelaba	nivelaban

	voy a nivelar	vamos a nivelar
	va a nivelar	van a nivelar

operar *(to operate)*

opero	operamos		operaba	operábamos
opera	operan		operaba	operaban

	voy a operar	vamos a operar
	va a operar	van a operar

pompear (to pump) Spanglish

pompeo	pompeamos		pompeaba	pompeabamos
pompea	pompean		pompeaba	pompeaban

	voy a *pompear*	vamos a *pompear*
	va a *pompear*	van a *pompear*

poner *(to put, to place)*

pongo	ponemos		ponía	poníamos
pone	ponen		ponía	ponían

	voy a poner	vamos a poner
	va a poner	van a poner

puchar (to push) Spanglish

pucho	puchamos		puchaba	puchabamos
pucha	puchan		puchaba	puchaban

	voy a *puchar*	vamos a *puchar*
	va a *puchar*	van a *puchar*

remover (ue) *(to remove)*

remuevo	removemos		removía	removíamos
remueve	remueven		removía	removían

	voy a remover	vamos a remover
	va a remover	van a remover

requear (to rake) Spanglish

requeo	requeamos		requeaba	requeabamos
requea	requean		requeaba	requeaban

	voy a requear	vamos a requear
	va a requear	van a requear

rufear (to roof) Spanglish

rufeo	rufeamos		rufeaba	rufeabamos
rufea	rufean		rufeaba	rufeaban

	voy a rufear	vamos a rufear
	va a rufear	van a rufear

sarapear (to set up) Spanglish

sarapeo	sarapeamos		sarapeaba	sarapeabamos
sarapea	sarapean		sarapeaba	sarapeaban

	voy a sarapear	vamos a sarapear
	va a sarapear	van a sarapear

seguir (i) *(to follow)*

sigo	seguimos	seguía	seguíamos
sigue	siguen	seguía	seguían

	voy a seguir	vamos a seguir
	va a seguir	van a seguir

ser *(to be)*

soy	somos	era	éramos
es	son	era	eran

	voy a ser	vamos a ser
	va a ser	van a ser

shiroquear (to sheetrock, to install sheetrock) Spanglish

shiroqueo	shiroqueamos	shiroqueaba	shiroqueábamos
shiroquea	shiroquean	shiroqueaba	shiroqueaban

	voy a *shiroquear*	vamos a *shiroquear*
	va a *shiroquear*	van a *shiroquear*

situar *(to situate, to place)*

sitúo	situamos	situaba	situábamos
sitúa	situan	situaba	situaban

	voy a situar	vamos a situar
	va a situar	van a situar

soportar *(to support)*

soporto	soportamos		soportaba	soportábamos
soporta	soportan		soportaba	soportaban

	voy a soportar	vamos a soportar
	va a soportar	van a soportar

startear (to start, to begin) Spanglish

starteo	*starteamos*		*starteaba*	*starteabamos*
startea	*startean*		*starteaba*	*starteaban*

	voy a *startear*	vamos a *startear*
	va a *startear*	van a *startear*

suspender *(to suspend, to hang)*

suspendo	suspendemos		suspendía	suspendíamos
suspende	suspenden		suspendía	suspendían

	voy a suspender	vamos a suspender
	va a suspender	van a suspender

taladrar *(to drill)*

taladro	taladramos		taladraba	taladrabamos
taladra	taladran		taladraba	taladraban

	voy a taladrar	vamos a taladrar
	va a taladrar	van a taladrar

teipear (to tape) Spanglish

teipeo	*teipeamos*		*teipeaba*	*teipeabamos*
teipea	*teipean*		*teipeaba*	*teipeaban*

voy a *teipear*	vamos a *teipear*
va a *teipear*	van a *teipear*

torcer (ue) *(to twist)*

tuerzo	torcemos		torcía	torcíamos
tuerces	**tuercen**		torcía	torcían

voy a torcer	vamos a torcer
va a torcer	van a torcer

traer *(to bring)*

tra**igo**	traemos		traía	traíamos
trae	traen		traía	traían

voy a traer	vamos a traer
va a traer	van a traer

unir *(to unite, to join, to connect)*

uno	unimos		unía	uníamos
une	unen		unía	unían

voy a unir	vamos a unir
va a unir	van a unir

usar *(to use)*

uso	usamos		usaba	usábamos
usa	usan		usaba	usaban

	voy a usar	vamos a usar
	va a usar	van a usar

Appendix B: Verb Rules

Even though our goal is to have some fun learning Spanish, every once in a while we have to take a pause and get a little boring for a few paragraphs. Starting with *regular* verbs, which are those nerdy ones that follow all the rules, the following will give you an overview of how Spanish verbs work. If any of this looks familiar, it's because we covered some of it when we introduced the forms of *necesitar*, your very first Spanish verb, in Section I. However, here's the thing—Don't try to memorize all the technical details right now. Just read the *Tackling "Regular" Verbs* material a couple of times to get a general feel for it. We will actually be using a different method for learning verbs, and once you have the hang of that, this other stuff will dovetail nicely without you having to worry about it.

TACKLING "REGULAR" VERBS

1. Verbs Ending in –ar

Since you already know and are using *necesitar*, which is an *-ar* type verb, let's use a different verb to give a brief reminder of how regular *-ar* verbs work. **Clavar**, *to nail*, should work fine for us here, and let me remind you again that this is a verb you gotta know!

Yo clavo *[yoh KLAHV-oh]*	*I nail, I am nailing*	clav + **o**
(Usted clava *[oo-STEHD* *KLAHV-ah]*	*You nail, you are nailing*	clav + **a**
El, ella clava *[ehl, EH-yah* *KLAHV-ah]*	*He, she nails, or* *is nailing*	clav + **a**

Nosotros
clavamos   *We nail, we are nailing*   clav + **amos**
[noh-SOH-tros
klahv-AH-mos]

Ustedes
clavan   *You guys nail, or*
[oo-STEHD-ehs *are nailing*   clav + **an**
KLAHV-ahn]

Ellos, ellas
clavan   *They nail,*
[EH-johs, EH-jahs *they are nailing*   clav + **an**
KLAHV-ahn]

If you look close, you will see that this works exactly the same as necesitar and every other regular –ar verb. Now is where it gets more interesting:

2. Verbs Ending in –er

One of the first things you may have noticed in the last section is that not all Spanish verbs end in the letters –ar, the way necesitar and clavar do. Most of the verbs we have given you do end in –ar, but some like *suspender* (to hang) end in –er, while a few verbs like *unir* (*to connect* or *join*) end in –ir. Don't panic, they are not really very different. Let's start by looking at an easy and useful –er verb like **barrer** *(bahrr-EHR)*, *to sweep*:

Yo barro   *I sweep, I am sweeping*   barr + **o**
(yoh BAHRR-oh)

Usted barre *You sweep, you are*
(oo-STEHD   *sweeping*   barr + **e**
BAHRR-eh)

Él, ella barre	*He, she sweeps, or*	
(ehl, EH-yah BAHRR-eh)	*is sweeping*	barr + **e**

Nosotros barremos	*We sweep, we are*	
(noh-SOH-tros bahrr-EH-mos)	*sweeping*	barr + **emos**

Ustedes barren	*You (plural) sweep, or*	
(oo-STEHD-ehs BAHRR-ehn)	*are sweeping*	barr + **en**

Ellos, ellas barren	*They sweep, they are*	
(EH-johs, EH-jahs BAHRR-ehn)	*sweeping*	barr + **en**

Look carefully, and you will see that, where **-ar** verbs end in **o, a, amos, an**, our friendly **-er** verbs end in **o, e, emos, en**. Pretty simple, huh? We use **a** for **-ar** verbs, and **e** for **-er** verbs. I am pretty sure you can remember this, even after a few cervezas. It ain't rocket science.

3. Verbs Ending in -ir

Verbs ending in *-ir* are basically wannabe -er verbs, with only one small exception. We'll use the verb **unir**, which you already know, for our example:

Yo uno	*I connect, I am*	
(yoh OO-noh)	*connecting*	un + **o**

Usted une	*You connect, you are*	
(oo-STEHD OO-neh)	*connecting*	un + **e**

El, ella une *(ehl, EH-yah* *OO-neh)*	*He, she connects, or is* *connecting*	un + **e**
Nosotros **unimos** *(noh-SOH-tros* *oo-NEE-mohs)*	*We connect, we are* *connecting*	un + **imos**
Ustedes unen *(oo-STEHD-ehs* *OON-ehn)*	*You (plural) connect,* *are connecting*	un + **en**
Ellos, **ellas unen** *(EH-yos, EH-yas* *OON-ehn)*	*They connect, are* *connecting*	un + **en**

If you look closely, you will see that the only difference between –er and –ir verb endings is in the "we" form, where –er verbs end in **emos** and –ir verbs end in **imos**; the other endings are exactly the same. So, in present tense, regular verbs, we have something that looks like the following:

	-AR VERBS like **clavar**	-ER VERBS like **barrer**	-IR VERBS like **unir**
YO (I)	o	o	o
USTED (you)	a	e	e
ÉL, ELLA (he, she)	a	e	e
NOSOTROS (we)	**amos**	**emos**	**imos**
USTEDES (you)	**an**	**en**	**en**
ELLOS (they)	**en**	**en**	**en**

An easy trick for remembering the right ending for "we" is that it is the same as the base verb. For an -ar verb, it's amos; for an -er verb, it's emos; and, for an -ir verb, it's imos.

While you are getting used to the other –ar and –er/-ir endings, you can start immediately taking advantage of the "we" form, because of this consistency. Using any or all of the verb infinitives you memorized in Section I, you can get your message across with the inclusive *we* form.

Excavamos las zapatas hoy.
We are digging the footings today.

Bueno. Ahora, borremos.
Good. Now we sweep up.

Mira. Los medimos, cortamos y clavamos.
Listen up. What we are going to do here is measure, cut and nail them.

LEARNING THOSE "NOT SO REGULAR" VERBS

This is a sneaky way of telling you that, like English, Spanish has a lot of verbs which are a wee bit *irregular* when it comes to the rules we just gave you. Most of the irregularities have to do with little differences in pronunciation (remember that languages were *spoken* for many years before anyone decided to try writing things down). By far the best way of learning these is to memorize them right the first time, and not worry about why they are the way they are. Appendix B contains an alphabetical listing of all the verbs introduced in this book, in our "visual graph" format; where a verb does not perfectly follow the rules, we have put the irregularities in **bold type** for easy identification and memorization. For now, just concentrate on the left column of Appendix B, which is the present tense of the verbs. We will get to the past and future of verbs as we go along.

The good news about Spanish is that most irregular verbs follow a few simple patterns—meaning that they are *regularly* irregular, if that oxymoron makes sense. There are three broad categories of verb irregularities:

Irregular Endings in the First Person "Yo" Form

To make the "Yo" form of a verb, we normally replace the -ar, -er, or –ir ending with an **"o"**, right? There are a small number of verbs where this changes a little bit, to **–go** or **–oy**, to assist pronunciation:

The important verb, **poner**, *to put* or *to place*, is a good example of the **–go** pattern:

pon**go**	ponemos
pone	ponen

Another important verb, **dar**, *to give*, will provide us with an example of the **–oy** pattern:

d**oy**	damos
da	dan

So-Called Stem-Changing Verbs

The part of the base verb, or *infinitive*, which remains when we remove the –ar, -er, or –ir ending is called the **stem**. As an example, for our favorite verb, necesitar, the stem is **necesit-**, and the ending is **–ar**. Some verbs with either an **e** or **o** vowel in the stem will either change the vowel or add another vowel. The three most common patterns are as follows:

e to i. An example of this pattern is the verb **pedir**, *to ask*. From pedir, we get:

p<u>i</u>do	pedimos
p<u>i</u>de	p<u>i</u>den

e to ie. An example of this pattern is the verb **pensar**, *to think*:

p<u>ie</u>nso	pensamos
p<u>ie</u>nsa	p<u>ie</u>nsan

o to ue. Our example is the verb *contar*, to count:

c**ue**nto	contamos
c**ue**nta	c**ue**ntan

Verbs with Spelling Changes

There are a number of verbs which appear to be irregular, due to certain spelling changes which mainly affect the first person singular *-o* form. These aren't actually irregular—the spelling changes are there to keep pronunciation more consistent—but still require special attention, because they don't *seem* to follow the rules. For example:

There are verbs ending in *-cer* and *-cir*, such as *conocer* or *conducir*. If you think way back to the pronunciation guide (Quickies 2), the letter c has the two sounds of k and s, depending on the vowel that follows. Because the c is followed by an e or i in these infinitives, the c takes the sound of s. The problem is that the first person singular is going to end in o, requiring a hard k sound, and, using *conocer* as our example, koh-NOH-**koh** doesn't sound much like koh-noh-**SEHR**. The answer is to slip in a z in front of the c in the first person singular of all these verbs, in order to add an s sound to the k—**conozco** (koh-NOH**S**-koh).

There is a similar problem with verbs ending with *-ger* and *-gir*, since the letter g also has a hard and soft pronunciation, depending on the vowel that follows (also in Quickies 2). The g has a soft sound in front of e and i, but a hard sound in front of the letter o. The answer to the problem is to trade the g for a j in the first person singular, in order to achieve the right sound. As an example, let's use *dirigir*, which is pronounced with a soft g in the infinitive, deer-ee-HEER. By substituting a j for the g in the first person, we get **dirijo** (deer-EE-hoh) instead of the hard **go** sound that we otherwise would get.

To learn Spanish verbs by memorizing the grammar rules and exceptions takes a lot of time, practice and patience. You can always buy a book of Spanish verbs, or learn to use the guides to irregular verbs found in most English/Spanish dictionaries, but it's a pain in the neck any way you look at it. This is why we recommend forgetting about all this and simply memorizing the verbs, one at a time, as they actually are.

Cognates

application	**aplicación**
association	**asociación**
authorization	**autorización**
circulation	**circulación**
classification	**clasificación**
combination	**combinación**
communication	**comunicación**
concentration	**concentración**
condensation	**condensación**
consideration	**consideración**
contamination	**contaminación**
continuation	**continuación**
conversation	**conversación**
cooperation	**cooperación**
corrosion	**corrosión**
determination	**determinación**
duration	**duración**

education	**educación**
elevation	**elevación**
elimination	**eliminación**
evacuation	**evacuación**
expansion	**expansión**
explanation	**explicación**
extension	**extensión**
foundation	**fundación**
identification	**identificación**
illumination	**iluminación**
illustration	**ilustración**
imagination	**imaginación**
information	**información**
installation	**instalación**
modification	**modificación**
occupation	**ocupación**
operation	**operación**
organization	**organización**
participation	**participación**
penetration	**penetración**

preparation	**preparación**
pronunciation	**pronunciación**
protection	**protección**
regulation	**regulación**
rehabilitation	**rehabilitación**
relation	**relación**
representation	**representación**
respiration	**respiración**
restoration	**restoración**
separation	**separación**
situation	**situación**
station	**estación**
tension	**tensión**
transportation	**transportación**
ventilation	**ventilación**

Other Useful Nouns

asphalt	**asfalto**
bunch	*bonche (Spanglish)*
cable	**cable**
cement	**cemento**

English	Spanish
chimney	**chimenea**
city	**ciudad**
color	**color**
concrete	**concreto**
conduit	**conducto**
coupling	**copla**
diagram	**diagrama**
distance	**distancia**
electricity	**electricidad**
error	**error**
experience	**experiencia**
form	**forma**
hatchet	**hacha**
hospital	**hospital**
knife	*naifa (Spanglish)*
line	**linea**
metal	**metal**
necessity	**necesidad**
paper	**papel**
pick (tool)	**pico**

plug	*ploga (Spanglish)*
post	**poste**
problem	**problema**
roof	*rufo (Spanglish)*
salary	**salario**
stake	**estaca**
stomach	**estómago**
structure	**estructura**
support	**soporte**
switch	*suiche (Spanglish)*
system	**sistema**
tape	*teip (Spanglish)*
tube (pipe)	**tubo** *(pipa – Spanglish)*
union	**unión**

Some Verb Cognates

to apply	**aplicar**
to authorize	**autorizar**
to calculate	**calcular**
to complete	**completar**

to concentrate	**concentrar**
to connect	**conectar**
to construct (build)	**construir**
to cut	**cortar**
to dump	*dompear (Spanglish)*
to demonstrate	**demonstrar**
to equal, to even	**igualar**
to escape	**escapar**
to estimate	**estimar**
to excavate (dig)	**excavar**
to flip (a switch)	*flipear (Spanglish)*
to haul	**jalar**
to ignore	**ignorar**
to install	**instalar**
to modify	**modificar**
to operate	**operar**
to organize	**organizar**
to prepare	**preparar**
to push	*puchar (Spanglish)*
to remove	**remover**

to repair	**reparar**
to set up	*sarapear [Spanglish]*
to simplify	**simplificar**
to solidify	**solidificar**
to support	**soportar**
to suspend	**suspender**
to use	**usar**
to utilize	**utilizar**

Some Adjectives

automatic	**automático**
effective	**efectivo**
electric	**eléctrico**
excellent	**excelente**
final	**final**
important	**importante**
impossible	**imposible**
local	**local**
necessary	**necesario**
negative	**negativo**
normal	**normal**

ordinary	**ordinario**
positive	**positivo**
primary	**primario**
secondary	**secundario**
solid	**sólido**
technical	**técnico**
terrible	**terrible**
usual	**usual**

A Few Adverbs

absolutely	**absolutamente**
completely	**completamente**
exactly	**exactamente**
finally	**finalmente**
naturally	**naturalmente**
normally	**normalmente**
rapidly	**rápidamente**
usually	**usualmente**

aplicación	employment application
ben	bin
bildin	building
bill	bill
bisi	busy
blokes, bloques	cinder blocks, blocks
bloquear	to block, to impede
boila	boiler
bompe	bump
bonche	bunch
break	break (rest period)
brekas	brakes
búngalo	bungalow, small house
cachar	to catch
carpeta	carpet
cash	cash
chance	maybe (by chance)
chatear	to chat

checar, chequear	to check, to analyze
chutar, chutear	to shoot
cilin	ceiling
clinap	clean up
cora	quarter (as in 25 cents)
corna	corner
craqueado	cracked
craquear	to crack, to break, to open
crashear	to crash, to collide
cuitear	to quit, to stop
culear	to cool
deal	deal
dealer	dealer, distributer
deliverar	to deliver
dimear	to dim
dompear	to dump
dona	donut
dúplex	duplex
escrachado	scratched

278

escrachar, escrachear	to scratch
eskipear	to skip
espray	aerosol, spray
feca	fake
fil	field
finishero	finish carpenter
flipear	to flip
freimero	framer
freimear, fremear	to frame
frihuey	freeway
frisar	to freeze
fuliar	to fool around
gasetería	gas station
grosería	grocery store
guachar	*see: wachar*
güinche	winch, crane
güindou	window
jaigüey	highway
jangear	to hang out

jira	heater, furnace
landsquipero	landscaper
laquear	to lock
liquear	to leak
livin	living room
lonche	lunch
lonchear	to have lunch
longo/a	length
loquear	to lock
loquer	locker
mapear	to mop
marqueta	market
mitin	meeting
mix	mix (mezcla)
mopa	mop
noquear	to knock
norsa	nurse
noujau	know-how
nursería	nursery (plants)

okey	O.K.
pantas	pants
parquear	to park
parqueo, parkin	parking lot
partaim	part-time
picap	pickup truck
pipisrúm	bathroom
ploga	plug
plomero	plumber
pompar, pompear	to pump
ponchar	to punch, to perforate
printear	to print
puchar	to push
raca	rack
raite	ride
raitear	to give a ride to
raitero	one who gives a ride to
rebildear	to rebuild
rentar	to rent

reque, reka	rake
requear	to rake
rufear	to roof
rufero	roofer
rufo	roof
sain, saine	sign
sharpenear	to sharpen
shiroquear	to install sheetrock, plasterboard
shiroquero	sheetrock installer
sink	sink
soda	soda, soft drink
spelear	to spell
startear	to start
suiche	switch
teip	tape
teipear	to tape
tiquete	ticket
trábol	trouble

tráila	big rig, semi, mobile home
trey	tray
troca	truck
vacunar, vaquear	to vacuum
van	van
wachar, güachar	to watch
waguina	station wagon
washatería	laundramat
yarda	backyard
yins	jeans
yob	job
yonque	wrecking yard
zíper	zipper

OTHER USEFUL SLANG

ahorita	Right now, right away
chafa	cheap
chále	no, no way
compa	friend, buddy
híjole!	man!

La Migra	INS (agents, the agency)
llamár pa'tras	to call back (telephone)
nones	no ("nope")
órale	yes (also: hi!)
pa'	short for **para** = *for*
pa'cá	short for **para acá** = *this way*
pa'ónde	short for **para dónde** = *where to?*
pa'rriba, p'arribera	short for **para arriba** = *upward*
pa'trás	short for **para atrás** = *backward*
símon	yes, yeah, yeah man

INDEX